Books in the

Let the Children Come Series

Let the Children Come Along the Infant Way
Let the Children Come Along the Toddler Way
Let the Children Come Along the Virtuous Way
Let the Children Come Along the Middle Years Way
Let the Children Come Along the Adolescent Way
Let the Children Come Along the Innocent Way

An Introduction to the

Let the Children Come *Series*

It's not an easy decision to make changes to a series of books that have impacted over three million parents and twice as many children. In fact it's risky. But as authors and publishers, we are willing to take this risk in order to bring greater continuity to our overall presentation of each curricula. It is our hope that this new look and approach to small group discipleship will help us further accomplish exactly what we set out to do over twenty years ago, to encourage, strengthen and help rebuild the Christian family to the glory of God.

Prior to the release of this series, Growing Families International offered the following parenting curriculums. *Preparation for Parenting; Preparation for the Toddler Years; Growing Kids God's Way; Preparation for Adolescence; Reaching the Heart of Your Teen;* and *Reflections of Moral Innocence*. In the past, the only thing that tied them together was a diamond shaped logo. Now, each title will be part of a single series entitled, *Let the Children Come*, bound together graphically and by a common title.

To our long time constituents, please know that our intent is not to eliminate the old titles but make them all members of a single series. *Reaching the Heart of Your Teen* will still be referred to as *Reaching the Heart of Your Teen* but now it is the fifth member in a six part series. *Growing Kids God's Way* will still be referred to as *Growing Kids God's Way*, but now it's the third member in the *Let the Children Come* series. While we will still randomly refer to each of the titles above in the audio and video presentation, they will textually also be referred to by their corresponding series name. Overall, it is the same hopeful message being delivered to a new generation of parents, repackaged to meet the changing needs of the ministry and our constituency.

Let the Children Come
Along the Adolescent Way

The companion workbook for the audio and video presentation
Reaching the Heart of Your Teen

Gary & Anne Marie Ezzo

Growing Families International
Presents

Let the Children Come Along the Adolescent Way
© 2002 Gary and Anne Marie Ezzo

International Standard Book Number

1-883035-05-8

Printed in the United States of America

Growing Families International
2130 Cheswick Lane, Mt. Pleasant, South Carolina 29466

03 04 05 06 07 — 6 5 4 3 2

Dedicated to:

Harold and Evelyn Duff
One weekend so many years ago

Acknowledgements

We owe a special debt of gratitude to a host of families who prayed us through the completion of this text. We want to especially thank Jeff and Sharon Secor for their ministry commitment to struggling teens and single parents and their ongoing encouragement to finish this project. Also, we wish to acknowledge Gary and Laurie Price, John and Holly–all who offer hope to many families because of the wonderful testimony of their own teenagers. We wish to thank Scott Shald for granting us permission to use the "Cat Street" story in our final challenge and closing remarks and Pastor Robert Boerman for his theological suggestions and contributions. Finally, we wish to thank Brenda Jackson for granting us permission to use her beautiful voice and the song "Loving Eyes" on the opening of *Reaching the Heart of Your Teen* audio and video presentations.

Table of Contents

Preface

When writing to express an idea, an author looks for words that will tie his thoughts together in a concise, coherent bundle. He does his best to use terms that will make his plea or point understood. But like life itself, which confounds our desire for fairy-tale endings, books about family renewal defy the use of simple categories. It will always be much easier to talk about healthy families and blissful parent-teen relationships than to achieve them. But please hear and believe this: Many healthy families exist. Within these pages, we will share with you the guiding principles that helped countless numbers achieve this status.

We are challenged by the variety of circumstances faced by moms and dads who will pick up this book. For some right now, the biggest challenge is to get their teen to turn off the bedroom light without being reminded. Others are faced with school and peer influences but no serious relational difficulty. Yet, many others are in open war with their teens and are deeply troubled–troubled to the point of despair. They are overwhelmed by the feeling that something has gone dreadfully wrong and are continually berated by an inner voice that relentlessly chants, "You are a failure." For them, the prospect of family renewal and friendship with an unmanageable teen seems nothing more than an impossible dream.

Whether you worry about your teen and dating or your teen and drugs, the principles to follow are appropriate and applicable for both extremes and everyone in between. *They do work!*

Each generation thinks their parenting problems are unique for their day and age. Be assured that no generation stands alone in their discouragement over the future. Just one generation ago, we heard how awful the teen years would be–a full-time headache, marked by impossible communication, peer-dependent children, rebellious behavior, and the end of domestic peace.

The warnings were endless: "If you're too strict, your children will rebel." "If you hold them to a standard, they will reject your values." "If you insist on compliance, you will only get opposition." "Enjoy your kids when they are young because it is not going to last!"

Dissatisfied but not surprised by the prevailing non Christian view of adolescence, we sought encouragement from within the Church. If there was any sense of hope, we reasoned, surely the Christian community would provide it. Yet we found many parents among church goers having their own teen-parent problems. We hopefully asserted that maybe we could do something as parents to avoid rebellion, drug use, and experimentation with sex by our teens. To this we received glares and frowns from mournful souls who rolled their eyes and offered the timeless warning: "You just wait."

We did wait. What we experienced with our teenage children was just the opposite of what was predicted by these prophets of pessimism. Looking back now, we would not trade those teen years for anything. They were not a disappointment, nor a disaster. They were delightful years—not perfect, but delightful nonetheless.

By the grace of God, we did not experience rebellion, sassy talk, doors slamming in defiance, threats to run away, or experimentation with drugs or sex. Not only was this period free of dominant negatives, it produced many positive. We were four individuals growing in our relationships. While accepting each other's human frailties, each one of us moved toward a greater love and loyalty within the special bond we call "family."

This book is not just our story; it is the story of many families who have experienced the joy of friendship with their teens. Although families such as ours appear to be a minority within our culture, we believe it is time that our voices be heard as an alternative to the disparaging message of the age. The stereotyping of teenagers as hopelessly stress-ridden, rebellious, anti-parent, and hormone-controlled might reflect more accurately society's moral ills than its will to change.

At the same time we do not dare boast in our accomplishments. We can give you satisfying food for thought, as well as practical help for building, maintaining, or even restoring painful relationships. But be assured, no family reaches a healthy status by its own power. There is a spiritual dimension that cannot be minimized. We serve a great God who is neither offended by our shortcomings nor weary of our cries for help. He does not grow impatient because we lost our way; He comes to us in time of need. Yes, if you need to, shout out just as Peter did on the sea, "Lord, save me!" He will come to save your family, to guide and direct you in His way. God is worthy of our hope; He alone brings renewal.

We would like to mention a few "housekeeping" details that apply to the structure of this manual. This workbook is incomplete without the corresponding video or audio tapes. To maximize learning, each parent should have his or her own book when going through the series.

We expanded this edition by adding Chapter 13, "Answering the Questions" As a result of our weekend conferences, letters from parents and inquires from leaders, we assembled the most popular questions asked of us. We trust this addition to the curriculum will further help bring clarity to the many challenges faced by parents today. We also added Chapter 14, "Dating, Courtship, and Marriage?" (The last chapter was formerly appendixes two and three.)

As it was previously, there are eight video sessions in this series. Each session is divided into two parts, both approximately thirty minutes long. The split session allows more time for discussion for those who choose to use the Sunday School hour for the class. Each session corresponds to a chapter (or chapters) in this workbook. Your standing homework assignment is to read the corresponding chapter(s) and answer the study questions at the end of each one. The match-up is as follows:

Session One
Part 1   The Healthy Family Profile . . . . .Chapter 1
Part 2   At the Heart of Rebellion . . . . .Chapter 2

Session Two
Part 1   The Power of Relationship . . . . .Chapter 3
Part 2   Starting Over with Credibility . . . . .Chapter 4

Session Three
Part 1   The Many Ways of Love . . . . .Chapter 5

Session Four
Part 1   From Authority to Influence . . . . .Chapter 6
Part 2   Principles of Moral Training . . . . .Chapter 7

Session Five
Part 1   Why Teens Don't Talk or Listen . . . . .Chapter 8
Part 2   Bridging the Communication Gap . . . . .Chapter 9

There are two matters of terminology we want to bring to your attention. First, we primarily use the masculine gender "he" throughout this book. This is done for convenience. The principles presented, of course, work equally well with both genders. Second, please note in the following pages, the word "we" refers to the collective insights of both authors. When referring to the experiences of just one partner, we have told the story from a third person perspective to avoid confusion about who is referred to by the word *I*.

May God bless your faithful work and sacrificial efforts toward the righteous upbringing of the next generation.

Gary and Anne Marie Ezzo
Charleston, South Carolina, 2002

and Chapter One & Two

The Healthy Family Profile

I. Welcome
   A. The Key Word is _____.
      1. Facing Reality
         We realize that some parents are participating in this series out of a sense of desperation. As it relates to your teen, the spirit of _____ is greater than the spirit of confidence.

      2. The objective of this class is to replace your fear with confidence and tension with _____.

   B. The Relational Continuum

   C. How Did We Get Here?

   The Three Funnels

      1. The _____ parenting funnel

Teens

Middle Years

Infancy & Toddler

2. The _____ parenting funnel

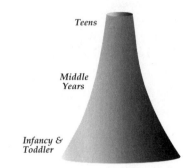

3. The _____ growth funnel

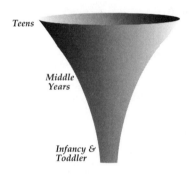

D. Where Should You Be?

"Henceforth, I no longer call you my servant, for a servant does not know what his master is doing. Now I call you friends, for all things that I have heard from my Father I have made known to you" (John 15:15).

E. Four Phases of Parenting

1. _____ phase

2. _____ phase

3. _____ phase

4. _____ phase

II. What is Teen rebellion?
  A. Teenage Rebellion Defined
     Teenage rebellion is culturally defined as a period of rebellion that is identified by our society as something _____ than the rebellion found in adults or small children.

     The Bible teaches that rejection of a higher authority at any age is rebellion. It is not limited to a function of the teen years.

  B. Popular Reasons for Teenage Rebellion

     1. _____

     2. _____

     3. _____

  C. The Source of Rebellion
     1. Where does teenage rebellion come from?
        Rebellion is a _____ issue.

     2. Young children rebel against authority; teenagers rebel against

        _____.

     3. Rejecting parental relationships is the lowest common denominator of the problem and the place where recovery starts. If you want to fix the problem or even prevent it, work on your relationships–not just a relationship, but a relationship that holds each family member accountable to common _____ system.

D. Summary Points: Negative Influences on Teen Relationships

1.

2.

3.

4.

5.

1

The Healthy Family Profile

A mong the Mundugumor people of New Guinea, there is a firm belief that children born with the umbilical cord wrapped around their necks are gifted by nature as artists. In this way, the Mundugumor society has connected two completely unrelated aspects of nature–a condition of birth and an ability to paint intricate designs on pieces of wood and stone. This belief is so woven into the fabric of social thought that people within the tribe who are born with the natural ability to paint, but had normal, uneventful births, seek out any trade but art. Such social conditioning is not completely unknown in our own society. Like the Mundugumor people, many in our culture automatically connect two unrelated subjects–teenagers and rebellion–then act on the belief that adolescence is a time of inevitable conflict. But is that really the case?

How would you describe the teen years? George Bernard Shaw once said, "Youth is a wonderful thing. What a crime to waste it on children." Mark Twain said that if he could, he would live his life over until he reached the age of fifteen... then he would drown.

A quick survey would most likely find parents using terms such as "difficult," "very stressful," and "tumultuous" to describe the teen-parenting experience. Parents today have little reason to believe a beautiful relationship lies waiting to be discovered during their children's teen years. Magazine articles and school counselors quote statistics about drug use, sexual activity, abortions, and violence that can leave us gasping, "Is it really that bad?" As if to confirm our worst fears, hardly a day passes without our local newspaper covering at least one story about a gang-related incident, the arrest of a teen for a violent crime, or a report on the decline of SAT scores.

In modern American society, it is a commonly held belief that parents and their teenagers will do battle. Pain, misery, and sorrow are accepted as a normal expression of family life in post-modern America. As we enter a new millium, teenage rebellion is widely seen as a normal and in some circles, even a healthy aspect of family life.

The fundamental problem with such descriptions of the present parent-teen experience is just that–they are simply *descriptions*. Statistics, surveys, and other clinical studies assume the validity of the power of observation. The process works this way: statistics tell us what is common; what is common then becomes what is normal; normal is deemed inevitable; and finally, what is seen as inevitable is labeled healthy. In fact, according to some psychologists the lack of teenage rebellion is a signal that something is terribly wrong with a child. Yet such logic is flawed. "Common" and "normal" are not interchangeable terms.

While we are well aware that most contemporary schools of parenting believe in the inevitability of the "storm and stress" years, we will tell you up front that we do not. Our message is very positive, upbeat, exciting, and comes with plenty of encouragement. We want parents to look forward to the fun-filled years of adolescence. Parents today have every reason to hope for and experience strong, positive, healthy, and lasting relationships with their teens. We did, and we want you to as well.

We do not write this book with an unsympathetic attitude toward those who may have struggled with their teenage kids. But we do write with the firm conviction that young parents are better served by encouragement instead of discouragement. We were badly misinformed about the teen years. We don't want you to be.

Why was our experience different from what we had been told to expect? First, we were not willing to accept the status quo that teens must rebel. That notion only causes parents to give up before they get started. Second, we believed with all our hearts that parents can and do make a difference because God makes a difference. And for those starting late, God can "restore to you the years that the swarming locust has eaten" (Joel 2:25). Third, we followed a basic strategy of observation. When our children were young, we made a habit of observing healthy families. By "healthy" we mean families that were characterized by a strong marriage, wonderful children, and a Christ-centered identity from which they developed a core of basic values. We carefully observed, followed, and asked questions of the families we wished to emulate.

We utilized the same strategy when writing *Along the Adolescece Way*. Just as we had done years earlier, we observed and spoke with families whose reputation for being "great families" with "terrific teens" was well-established in their communities. We concentrated on learning what they did as families that set them apart from the norm, and we examined how they lived the truth of Jesus Christ every day. It is from this positive, victorious perspective and experience that we write this volume.

We'll tell you up front that parenting a teenager takes work, diligence, and patience. Most importantly, it will require taking a new and honest look at yourself. The cycle of change begins with parents. Yet the rewards are far-reaching. Our desire for this book is not to make you a better parent or your teen a better son or daughter, but to help all of you become better people—people who know Christ, and understand His mind, purpose, and plan for enduring relationships. These are the threads from which God weaves strong families.

ADOLESCENCE PAST AND PRESENT

Every species, whether animal or human, follows a pattern of development peculiar to that species. That is God's design. For every human adult, there is a period of eight or nine years when that person is no longer a child but not yet an adult. Adolescence is the term used to designate this in-between period of life. The word is derived from the Latin verb *adolescere*, meaning to ripen, or grow into maturity. Adolescence is a period of growth when the characteristics of childhood are gradually exchanged for those of adulthood—a time when a child is not firmly established in either category.

There is a difference between the terms adolescent and teen. The word "teen" (or "teenager") is derived from the numerical age span of thirteen to nineteen years, while "adolescent" is a broader term. A child enters adolescence with the onset of puberty, which occurs between ten and twelve years of age, and ends with physical maturity, usually attained between the years of nineteen and twenty-one. The Bible doesn't use the terms "adolescent," "adolescence," or "teenager," but refers to children of this approximate age as youths or young men. For example, Daniel, Shadrach, Meshack, and Abed-Nego were all "young men" when taken to Babylon to serve Nebuchadnezzar (Daniel 1:3-4). Bible scholars place their ages between twelve and fifteen years. David is thought to have been about this same age when he fought Goliath as a "youth" (1 Samuel 17:42).

Regardless of which term is used—"teenager," "adolescent," "young man," or "youth"—each of these words represents essentially the same period of growth and development. In this series we will use the terms interchangeably and in the context of our society.

THE CHALLENGE OF ADOLESCENSCE

There are well-adjusted adolescents and not so well-adjusted ones. There are teens who have a coherent sense of purpose and others who are desperately seeking one. There are plenty of pro-parent young people around, and there are those whose relationships with their parents are sadly deficient. We will begin to discuss the reasons for these two very different sets of conclusions.

The period of development known as adolescence has been part of the human scene for a long time. To some extent, every generation has faced the challenges of adolescence. Socrates, Aristotle, St. Augustine, and even William Shakespeare spoke of it. As late as 1828, Noah Webster's *American Dictionary of the English Language* defined "adolescence" as the state of growing in the period of life between childhood and manhood. Webster defined "teen" as pertaining to the period of time spanning the years thirteen to nineteen. Both of these definitions, approximately 175 years old, describe what we today call adolescence.

As we close out this century, our society confronts adolescence with a well-established belief that this period is peculiarly troublesome. In 1904, G. Stanley Hall wrote what was considered the definitive work on the psychology of adolescence. In his book, *Adolescence*, he concluded that the period was a time of "storm and stress" characterized by teens running the gamut of emotional expressions. His work established the psychological norm for the next ninety years.

In 1961, James Coleman added to that sinking stereotype. His book, *The Adolescent*, popularized the theory that peer pressure renders parents voiceless and helpless, unable to cope with the power of peer influence on their teen. Coleman's characterization of adolescent behavior so stereotypes teenagers that now, nearly forty years later, blissful teen-parent relationships can only be classified as an unexpected outcome. When such healthy relationships do occur, they are explained away as developmental flukes, family oddities that are highly suspect, and impossible to duplicate.

Psychologist Erick Erikson considered adolescence to be a period of "normative crisis." Anna Freud insisted that lack of stress during adolescence was an anomaly and therefore a cause for concern! From her psychoanalytical standpoint, something must be wrong if things are going well between parent and teen. Unfortunately, even some youth pastors and youth workers accept and thus perpetuate this negative stereotype consistent with secular thought.

More than ever, parents today are demoralized by clichés, slogans, and negative public examples–all adding up to a psychological warfare of despair. There is no conspiracy on the part of public voices to demoralize an entire generation of new parents, but that is exactly what is happening. Young parents are brought to the point of despair by statements such as these: "All teens rebel, you just wait." Or, "Enjoy them now; you won't when they're teens." Or, "You can't stop teens from doing drugs and having sex. You just have to let them do what they want." Not only are young parents deeply discouraged by clichés and negative slogans, but resulting defeatist attitudes inevitably lead to self-fulfilling conclusions.

This attitude of defeat has so permeated our society that parents today are becoming apathetic. Just as the cloud ceiling drops with the approaching storm, so also the ceiling of despair descends on an entire generation. For most parents, the real tragedy is that there is no storm on the horizon except the one created in their own minds by fear and doubt. Do you remember the Mundugumor tribe mentioned in chapter one? Parents' willingness to accept defeat without even attempting to confront the imagined foe could be described as a "Mundugumor tribe experience."

No wonder young parents are skeptical when they hear the occasional voice proclaiming positive things about parent-teen relations talking about such things as "terrific teens" instead of terrible, peace in the home rather than war, cooperation instead of conflict, love between family members instead of hostility, and hope instead of despair. But be encouraged. In spite of the pessimistic predictions which prevail, one fact remains: You can have a great relationship with your teen. Don't accept adolescent struggles as inevitable, and don't wait for the transformation of society to help make your job easier. Parents are always in a position to make a difference. The fact is, you are in the process of making a difference right now.

ENOUGH BLAME TO GO AROUND

As we travel from city to city leading parenting conferences, it seems like the only thing on our itinerary that changes is the names and faces of hurting parents. Feeling confused and betrayed, they share a common story. "We don't understand! Bobby was raised in the church from the time he was born. We sent him to a Christian school. He participated in all the youth programs. But now as a teenager, he has rejected our values. Why?"

What would cause a teen to reject the strong relational values taught him in early life? There are many answers to that question, but at the top of the list should be something the Bible calls *depravity* (Isaiah 53:6). Man knows what is right but still he chooses to go his own way. Other reasons for the abandonment of values include fear (2 Timothy 1:7), loneliness (2 Timothy 4:16), greed (1 Timothy 6:9-10), immorality (1 Timothy 4:12 and 2 Timothy 6:9-10), legalism (1 Timothy 4:3-4), and disillusionment that Christianity does not deliver what was promised (1 Timothy 6:5-10). The apostle Paul saw many people defecting from the faith and listed the above as some of the reasons why people drift away from God. Some may be the same reasons teens drift away from their parents.

There are other factors that may lead teens to abandon the security of their parents' love. We live in a society that is fundamentally hostile toward the family. Concerned parents who want to raise good children are virtually at war with the community. This was not always the case. Fifty years ago a shared Judeo-Christian ethic produced a social harmony and unity that is no longer experienced today. At that time, even bad parents could raise good children because the society had safety nets in place to pick up the slack when moms and dads failed. If a teen had a negligent parent during the 1950s, neighbors, teachers, little league coaches, and the community at large provided the moral direction the child was lacking. This happened because communities operated from one set of values. All values had common meaning; nothing was relative.

Today we live in a society that believes that *morals* are relative. Therefore, as a result, common moral communities are virtually nonexistent. That is why today you can be a good parent and still turn out a wayward child. Without a moral community surrounding and upholding your values, you fight alone against lude television programming, pornography, drugs, premarital sex, crude public advertising, values-based education, degrading schools, and negative peer pressure. A parent can get really depressed when listing the moral differences between our homes and our communities.

Still, there *is* a parent factor to consider in confronting teenage rebellion. The period of adolescence is the culmination of all that has gone on before in a child's life. All interaction between parent and child in the formative years–right or wrong, the result of intent or neglect–strongly shapes the social and relational characteristics of the child before he or she becomes a teen. This can be a frightening thought for parents. Realization that the thread of adolescent behavior is tied either to adequate or faulty training in early childhood (and in many cases, if no correction or encouragement comes, it will extend into adulthood) is a sobering thought, to say the least.

Having stated that, we wish to move forward. As far as we are concerned, there is no need to dwell on what did not happen but rather, what can still happen under my influence. We have all made similar mistakes. That was yesterday, and today is a new day. We all need a fresh start. Thankfully, our God is the God of new beginnings. The problems you might be facing may be the result of sin on the part of you, your teen, your community, or a combination of all three. Regardless of the source of the rebellious influence, the starting point for renewal and healing will always be the same—your relationship with your teen.

A TWO-EDGED SWORD

No one who believes in Christian charity wishes to inflict more pain upon those who are grieving over their children's or their own troublesome choices in life. Such compassion leads many of us to speak these words to parents: "It's okay; it is not your fault; you are not to blame." Yet these reassurances are like the blade of a two-edged sword. The sweeping cut that so neatly divides personal responsibility from happenstance at the same time severs hope from despair. If pure motives without right methods render us blameless for what we do or say, then we have no hope of recovering from destructive patterns of parenting. But this is not the case. We, as parents, must know that our actions do have an impact.

Thus, words intended to extend loving encouragement may offer false comfort. We do no favors for this generation nor for future generations by consoling with words of goodwill while shielding those we wish to help from the truth.

Secular and Christian counselors alike recognize the untold damage that is done to society and to an individual when personal responsibility is undermined. We live in a day marked by a victimization epidemic. The truth is, in most people-to-people situations, we are at once victim and agent.

Some children are victims of poor parental choices. Yet it is equally true that they are themselves agents of sinful choices as well. A balanced, biblical view would have both parent and child taking responsibility for their own actions. Somehow, in the confluence of activity of parent and child, each will have responsibility for their own actions and thus in some ways, responsibility for the life of the other.

Where Are We Today?

As we confront our hearts, we'll need to look at our ideas about adolescence, our pasts, our parenting styles, and elements that improve and maintain relationships. But first, we must take an honest look at our current relationships.

In order to help you, we've put together forty questions that are designed to assess your parent-teen relationships. Answering these questions honestly won't be easy. From hundreds of questionnaires completed by parents across the country, we discovered that the families with a public "healthy" reputation tended to be harder on themselves, earning higher scores than those that reflected their real situation. Conversely, struggling families tended to under rate the seriousness of their problems or contradicted themselves. Some answered, "Yes, my son is on drugs," but also answered, "Yes, my son is a strong Christian." It hurts to give answers that drive home the reality of a poor or struggling relationship between you and your teen. But there is also great hope in beginning the process. In order to gain optimum help, please be as honest as you can.

The scores at the conclusion of the test represent actual readings from families who have both a private and public reputation as being:

1. Strong families with healthy parent-teen relationships.
2. Surviving families who could benefit from improvement and who may experience significant problems in the future.
3. Struggling families with parent-teen relationships characterized by serious conflict.

The test is designed simply to provide you with an objective point of reference. Your final score will help you evaluate where you stand. The test is not meant to encourage or discourage you (although both may happen), but to provide a starting point for improvement. Remember, a stronger relationship with your teen is your goal.

One Final Word of Encouragement

Before you begin, let us remind you of the remarkable freedom and hope that come with exacting honesty. Bible scholars tell us that the term *confession* means to "say the same thing as." It is critical for us to understand that turning from a destructive pattern to a life-giving pattern of living begins with a bold and thoughtful look at reality.

We want to encourage you that you do not have to fear that process. The door to healing is unlocked by the key marked "Honesty." Remember, just on the other side of that door is a merciful Father. There is no better time to begin. So go ahead and commit your heart to the Lord, take the test once for each teen in your home, and get ready to begin the process of healing your relationship with your teen!

HEALTHY FAMILY PROFILE

This test is divided into two sections, each with a different rating scale. Please note the difference when you go to the second section. After completing both sections, add the scores, total the results, and mark them on page 27. If for some reason a question does not apply, make an educated guess. For personal enlightenment, consider taking the test on behalf of your own parents. How do you think they would answer these questions about you?

Section One

Write your responses in the spaces adjacent to each question in this section, basing your answers on the following 1 to 5 scale:

1 = This represents our teen or our relationship.
2 = This usually represents our teen or our relationship.
3 = Sometimes this is true of our teen or our relationship, but just as often it is not.
4 = This is not usually true of our teen or our relationship.
5 = This rarely, if ever, is true of our teen or our relationship.

1 ___ Our parent-teen communication is characterized by very few limitations. We can talk about anything.
2 ___ Our teen looks forward to special family times when it is just us together.
3 ___ Our teen's friends consider our family a fun family to be with.
4 ___ Our teen considers us to be a good source of counsel.
5 ___ Our teen can accept "no" for an answer without blowing up.
6 ___ Peer pressure has less influence on our teen than we do.

7 ___ Our teen is interested in what is going on in our lives.

8 ___ When our teen comes home late, we know he/she will have a legitimate reason.

9 ___ Our teen would be one of the sources of counsel that we would seek out in times of crisis.

10 ___ When we have a disagreement with our teen, we make up quickly with out harboring a grudge.

11 ___ Our teen knows that if we wrong him/her in any way, he/she can count on an apology from us.

12 ___ If we were running late and left the dinner dishes on the table, our teen would probably clean the table, wash the dishes, and put them away.

13 ___ Our teen considers us to be fair and flexible.

14 ___ Our teen accepts criticism, evaluates it, and is willing to talk about it.

15 ___ Our teen considers us to be part of his/her inner circle of best friends.

16 ___ Our teen picks up after him or herself.

17 ___ If our teen had a choice, he/she would choose us to be his/her parents.

18 ___ Our friends enjoy our teen.

19 ___ Our teen has his/her own quiet time with the Lord. We don't have to prompt him/her.

20 ___ Our teen feels appreciated by us.

Now add up all of the numbers you placed in the blanks above and enter your score here: Section One Score _____

Section Two

Write your responses in the blanks adjacent to each question in this section, basing your answers on the following 5 to 1 scale.

5 = Always true, or this is very representative of our teen, his/her feelings, our feelings, or our relationship.

4 = Often the case, or this is usually representative of our teen, his/her feelings, our feelings, or our relationship.

3 = Sometimes this is true, but just as often it is not.

2 = This happens but not often. Or, this is not usually representative of my teen, his/her feelings, our feelings, or our relationship.

1 = This is rarely, if ever, true of our teen or our relationship.

1 ___ When we ask our teen to do something, we always seem to end up in a power struggle.

2 ___ Our teen prefers spending more time with his/her friends than with our family.

3 ___ Our teen will often agree with what we say but then do what he/she wants.

4 ___ Our teen is easily influenced by his/her peers or trendy styles or behaviors.

5 ___ Setting limits on our teen doesn't do any good. He/She ignores them all.

6 ___ Our teen cannot wait to grow up and leave our home.

7 ___ Our teen is not sought out as a babysitter.

8 ___ For his/her age, we don't feel confident in our teen's ability to make wise age-appropriate decisions for him or herself.

9 ___ If we get into an argument, our teen may not talk to us for a couple of days.

10 ___ If it weren't for sports or the weather, we probably wouldn't have any thing to talk about with our teen.

11 ___ We're fearful that our teen is experimenting or has experimented with drugs.

12 ___ Our teen has little interest in spiritual things.

13 ___ Our teen's taste in clothing and hair style is totally opposite of ours.

14 ___ If we were going away for the weekend, I don't think we could trust our teen to stay home alone.

15 ___ Our teen puts stress on the whole family.

16 ___ We are fearful that if we place too many demands on our teen, he/she will run away.

17 ___ Our teen physically threatens us.

18 ___ We're fearful that our teen is sexually active or even promiscuous.

19 ___ Our teen has the attitude that everyone else can pick up after him/her.

20 ___ Our teen thinks we are overly critical of him/her.

Section Two Score   _____

Section One Score   _____

Grand Total   _____

Compare your score to the numbers posted under the Family Profile Summary below.

Family Profile Summary

40 – 60	Very healthy parent-teen relationship.
61 – 80	Healthy parent-teen relationship with minor problems.
81 – 115	Okay-to-weak parent-teen relationship. There are some behavioral concerns that, if not corrected, can lead to struggles and conflict.
116 – 140	Weak parent-teen relationship characterized mostly by conflict.
141 – 170	Barely tolerable parent-teen relationship.
171 – 190	Parent-teen relationship is nonexistent.

Name of Teen _____

Score _____

Name of Teen _____

Score _____

Name of Teen _____

Score _____

2

At the Heart of Rebellion

It is normal from time to time for all of us to have bad days with our kids. But how does your typical day go? Are you faced continually with the realization that something has gone wrong? How do you respond when your friends inquire about your family and ask, "So, how's life with a teenager?"

When it comes to explaining things, people can get very creative. Just take these notes sent to excuse students from school:

- Please excuse Johnnie for being. It was his father's fault.
- George was absent yesterday because he had a stomach.
- Please excuse Sara for being absent. She was sick and I had her shot.
- Ralph was absent yesterday because he had a sore trout.

There are just as many theories out there to explain why teenagers go astray. A few are as imaginative as the excuses above. Some minimize it by saying it's just disagreement. Is it? There is a big difference between the terms disagreement and rebellion. *Disagreement* refers to a difference of opinion. *Rebellion* denotes acts and attitudes intended to change or overthrow family government and replace it with self-government–a concept incompatible with family harmony. To be in a protracted state of rebellion is to be in a state of war.

Some people say rebellion is caused by hormones; some say it's caused by the media; some say it's just a natural part of growing up. We hear it must be genetics or a lack of self-esteem or the result of some exotic syndrome. It's parents' too-strict limitations that have caused the behavior–or the lack of any restraint whatsoever. It's because he was underattached, overattached, or the newest of excuses, wasn't breast-fed or breast-fed long enough. Or it's the result of improper self-discovery or a fear of abandonment caused by that time you left him with the sitter when he was two.

Some of these explanations seem to be attempts by parents to evade responsibility for their teen's misbehavior. Others seem to say that the parents are completely to blame, and the poor child is just misunderstood. How can we separate the silver from the dross?

We'll take a look at these theories in a moment. First, let's examine what teen rebellion (we prefer the term *relational tension*) looks like. Once you learn to recognize it, you're well on the way to dealing with it.

When we talk about relational tension in teenagers, we mean the teen displays a willful desire to overthrow family leadership, or a willingness to walk away from relational accountability or both. Relational tension, though it may have many external influences, ultimately arises from human nature. The Bible points us back to our own hearts.

Relational tension whether it be with a parent, sibling, or another member of the worlds population is clearly the result of our fallen humanity (Psalm 51:5). It is the absence of wisdom ruling the moment (Proverbs 1:7, 26:12). It is man saying "No" to God, His ways, and His precepts (Romans 3:18). It is uncorrected foolishness that was bound up in the heart of the child (Proverbs 22:15).

All of us want to get our way. When some power or authority comes in and thwarts us from having our way, we get mad. We fight to overcome that force so that we can get what we want. Each of us handles this conflict differently.

Some struggle with the force that opposes them, but when it cannot be overcome, they comply. Others, when they come to the realization that they can't defeat the authority, flee. Those who flee are usually running from one of three things: a social obligation, a responsibility, or a relationship. Teenagers tend to flee from relationships, which comes out in the form of rebellion.

Even if your teen is a regular in the principal's office or is having run-ins with the police, we believe the ultimate source of the relational tension is a deficiency in the parent/teen relationship. If that's not healthy, teens will rebel against it, and a host of other problems will logically follow.

Nevertheless, parents tend to look for other explanations for their teen's behavior, things that will show that it wasn't anything they've done or failed to do. Let's look at some of the candidates.

THE USUAL SUSPECTS
When a crime is committed by an unknown assailant in a high-crime district, the police pull in the usual suspects for questioning and for a witness lineup.

Many times the real culprit isn't among that group, after all, but it's always a good place to start.

So now, when we're trying to deduce who or what is responsible for teenage rebellion, we're going to haul in the usual suspects—the explanations usually offered—for examination. We don't believe the offender is here, but since these are such popular answers in our society, we thought this would be a good place to start.

THE BIOLOGICAL DIMENSION

Your fourteen-year-old son is starting to pay more attention to his grooming because of a dawning attraction to the opposite sex. His preferences in music and hairstyle are beginning to reflect what his peers like more than what you like. You're beginning to have conflict over his after-school whereabouts. You want him home working on his school projects; he wants to be at the mall. His attitude and tone toward you have changed for the worse. The battles have begun, and back and forth you go.

Your fifteen-year-old daughter feels bloated during her period. She's become dissatisfied with her appearance and is pushing herself into a semistarvation pattern of eating. Alarmed at her weight loss, you try to force her to eat. This just pushes her to go throw up when she thinks you don't know. Tension builds and daily arguments ensue.

Is testosterone to blame for your son's attitude problems? Are hormones making your daughter a little crazy? Tantrums, defiance, eating disorders—indeed, all the problems commonly encountered in adolescence—are often explained away as the result of hormonal changes in a young person's body. It's the terrible twos back with a wallop. Their poor behavior is excused as completely natural, just a phase all teens have to go through. But is this really what is at the root of the trouble? American society would say yes. We say, probably not.

To be sure, hormones are operating in overdrive during the teen years. They do affect behavior and attitudes to some degree. But the crucial question is this: Do hormonal changes cause your children to make bad choices?

We should point out that there are legitimate medical problems associated with hormonal imbalances. An excess or deficiency of one or more of the hormones produced by the glands of the endocrine system can affect personality. A hyperthyroid condition, for example, can make a child nervous, excited, jumpy, restless, and overactive. A hypothyroid condition, on the other hand, causes children to be lethargic, unresponsive, dissatisfied, even depressed.

Nor are teens the only ones affected by hormones. Just consider a woman in menopause. She will experience hot flashes, sweating, dryness, burning, and itching–all legitimate results of hormonal change. But if this forty-something mother of three tossed her apron, hopped on a Harley, and headed for Alaska, could she blame it on hormones? No. She would be making a choice. Her actions would have happened during the midst of hormonal flux, but they would hardly have been caused by it.

Nevertheless, some parents make the same mistake, blaming their teen's misbehavior on hormonal changes that happened at the same time as their misbehavior but which were not the cause of it.

Supporters of the hormone-induced rebellion theory suggest that hormonal changes substantially increase a teen's tendency to rebel and reject the values of his or her family. They almost seem to believe that what the endocrine system produces is not estrogen or testosterone but pure, liquid defiance–rebellion juice.

If it were true that the endocrine system's release of hormones into the body automatically triggered rebellion, then this kind of rebellion would begin at age seven since that's when hormonal changes begin. The new growth period marks the end of a hormonal suppression set in place soon after birth and the beginning of many years of glandular arousal. At age seven, the gonadotrophin hormone levels begin to rise in both boys and girls. By age twelve this process has been in full swing for several years. Therefore, if a child hits twelve or thirteen and suddenly starts defying authority, there is no reason to blame hormones.

Glandular surges do not cause children to lie, steal, cheat, act disrespectfully, defy authority, or relationally wander away from their parents. Hormones may affect the human body, but not the human heart.

If hormones caused rebellion:

- the problem would be universal. The genetic time clock would kick in at essentially the same time for children in all societies and cultures, bringing about rebellion in adolescents across the globe. Just the thought of it would keep us awake nights. Thankfully, it doesn't happen this way.

- how do we explain the healthy families whose teens don't rebel? These kids go through the same hormonal changes but do not seek to overthrow their parents' leadership.
- why isn't medication its cure?

Hormones are unquestionably at work during the teen years. They add to the energy and awkwardness and even stress of adolescents. But they should not be allowed to excuse bad behavior any more than having a bad day at work excuses child abuse. Teenagers retain their ability–and their responsibility–to make good choices and keep their attitudes in check.

A SEARCH FOR INDEPENDENCE
You and your thirteen-year-old daughter seem to clash all the time these days. You've heard that daughters just have to disagree with mothers as part of growing up, and you remember something from psychology class that says sons have to "murder" the father figure to become men themselves. So you're pretty sure that the constant disagreements with your own teen are just a case of her seeking to become her own person, separate from her parents.

The theory goes like this: Adolescence is the period when children attempt to separate themselves from the parental bonds of love and dependence and move toward an adult identity. It is another attempt to explain why a teenager would close his or her heart toward Mom and Dad during the teen years. These kids aren't rebelling, the theory goes, they're simply striving for independence. They are "planting their flag," declaring themselves independent and sovereign. This tearing away is said to be necessary in order for the child to become an adult.

In one sense, this is certainly true: A teenager is experiencing a rebirth. He is coming out of the cocoon of childhood and beginning to explore his world and his self. He's considering for himself who he wants to be rather than simply being a child. He's able to make informed decisions, decisions that may differ from what his parents would choose. He's seeking independence from the things of childhood. There is an invigorating sense of self-determination during the teen years in which the young person feels he is master of his own destiny.

Is adolescence really just one continuous, unavoidable struggle filled with endless conflict until independence is achieved? At that point, does the prodigal son or daughter miraculously return home, endearing him or herself to mom and dad? What part does nurture play? Let's look at this further.

Defining Independence

We wish we could find another term to use other than independence, because in popular discussion, the word often has the connotation of defiance. To be independent basically means to lack dependence. Clearly, man isn't an island and is always dependent in one way or another upon others. In the Christian world and life view, this dependency is both vertical and horizontal. We are forever dependent upon God. "Without me you can do nothing" Christ said (John 15:5). It is equally true that a believer cannot be all that God intends him to be without the regular and meaningful contributions of other members of the Body of Christ (see Romans 12, 1 Corinthians 12, Ephesians 4). Thus independence is both practical or righteous necessity.

The independence notion is rooted in the Freudian theory of the personality. According to Freud, a child's quest to be detached from parental control is the root cause of teenage rebellion. And since Freud's legacy is alive and well today, many parents now believe that rebellion isn't a question of *if* but of *when*.

The idea that rebellion is necessary in order for a child to become an adult offers a false sense of comfort to bewildered parents, freeing them from account-ability for their teen's behavior. However, it also can discourage parents, causing many to give up before they start. If parents believe that no matter what they do in the early years, conflict is unavoidable, it adds up to a lose-lose situation for the family.

Teens do, in a good sense and as part of the maturation process, seek independence. That's a fact of life. But from what are they seeking independence? That question is central to understanding the issues at hand. Through our examination of healthy families, we have found that the quest for independence finds the teen moving away from his childhood and childhood structures, not from relationships with his parents. In strong families, teens *transform* their relationships with their parents; not abandon them. Earlier, we addressed the fallacious assumption of "inevitable-rebellion." Certainly, sin and its effects permeate everything we are and do. Our bodies, our relationships, our emotions, and our reason are impacted by sin. Thus, we are not so naive as to think that families can avoid problems altogether.

What we *are* saying is that teenage rebellion is not an unavoidable experience. Sin affects marriages as well. Statistically, divorce is very common. However, couples do not and should not see divorce as inevitable. Our God is bigger than that. In the same way, we need not expect that growth from childhood to adulthood results in a fracturing of the relationship between the teen and parent.

We mentioned that in strong families teens seek to separate themselves from their childhood structures, but what about struggling families? From what are those teens seeking independence? As in the previous example, these teens seek independence from childhood and early structures of growth and development. But this is not the sole issue for them; they also seek independence from unhealthy relationships.

When a fledgling teen is presented with a too strict confinement or no loving boundaries; when house rules are required for the kids but not for the parents; when parental hypocrisy causes communication to be less than honest; when the parents' marriage is in a continual state of conflict–then, yes, there is a high probability that the teen will seek to break ties with the family. He or she does so to escape pain, hypocrisy, love's neglect, or parental dominance, but not because of some preprogrammed genetic time cue that sends him off in search of independence.

Under these circumstances, parents, as well as childhood peers, are the focus of a child's quest for freedom. The unhealthy aspects of their relationship drive the teen away from his parents, just as they would in any relationship. Hence, the teen sets himself against his parents, their ideals, and their values. Is this condition repairable? Yes, that is the good news for the Christian. The entire message of God's love is one of reconciliation. In later chapters we will discuss the how-tos of family renewal.

Bottom line? Teens don't have to become something their parents dislike in order to be their own individuals. If that were so, a teen wouldn't be unique; he would just be a mirror image of his parents. If Mom and Dad were conservative, Junior would *have* to be liberal, or he would just be his parents' clone. We don't think it has to be this way. Teens do need to find out who they want to be, but they should be free to select qualities and values held by their parents as well as those not held by them.

In our opinion, reaching adulthood does not require relational tension. Defiance of authority is not a growing pain but a behavioral choice. Rebelling against parents doesn't make you an adult any more than rebelling against a government makes you president.

SELF-ESTEEM: THE CAUSE OR EFFECT?

A third theory often given for why teenagers rebel involves the role of self-esteem. Many believe that a lack of positive self-esteem is the root cause of teens doing drugs, experiencing academic failure, participating in gang violence, becoming sexually active, and rebelling against their parents.

In America, self-esteem enhancement is everywhere. We read about it, hear it over the radio, watch it on sitcoms, learn it in the classroom, and move to its music. Contemporary sociologists, psychologists, and educators alike say that a child's happiness, success, physical coordination, and, yes, even IQ hinge upon a healthy self-esteem.

Two sets of words immediately come to mind when defining in contemporary terms what is meant by self-esteem: *self-approval* and *self-validation*. Both are fairly descriptive titles of what educators are hoping to accomplish with children through self-esteem training. As used in our modern vernacular, esteem as a noun means "favorable opinion." *Self-esteem* means "favorable opinion of self."

The idea that children will possess an abiding favorable opinion of self, and that this leads to a better life is popular. And for sure self-esteem plays a role. A teen who feels worthless is likely to act out in any number of disruptive ways. (On the other hand, a teen who feels superior to everyone else is just as unpleasant to be around.) But wait: Does a poor self-esteem excuse defiant, disrespectful, or illegal actions? Should someone be acquitted of a crime because he was feeling bad about himself when he committed it? Is *feeling good* the prerequisite for *doing good*?

Parents working under the theory that self-esteem is the Holy Grail of child-rearing become slaves to whatever it takes to make the child feel good about himself. They work tirelessly to ensure that children have the right activities, the right clothes, the right car, the biggest party, a "cool" dad who lets anything go, and the "supermom" who strives to create utopia for the kids. Parents feel they must maximize the child's pleasure and minimize his pain, or he'll end up being a menace to society.

If the child's got to feel good before he'll act correctly, all misbehavior is really the parent's fault. If he throws his cereal bowl on the carpet, it's because Mommy hasn't made him feel happy. If she looks right at you while doing something you told her not to, it's your fault somehow. No wonder parents are enslaved to keeping their children appeased: They perceive misbehavior as parental failure.

To be fair, most parents who ascribe to this theory love their children greatly and sincerely think this is the way to help them succeed in life. Parents often strive selflessly to make sure their children have what they need for healthy self-esteem. But gallant as this effort may be, we still have to ask if it was necessary in the first place. It may seem heroic to dive into a pool after a drowning child, but any lifeguard will tell you that using a long pole would have been smarter.

Does good self-esteem produce healthy development in children, or does healthy development produce within children a satisfying sense of self? If it's the former, then mainstream America is right in its efforts to enhance warm fuzzies. But if the latter is true, if indeed the effort to raise self-esteem is actually contributing to America's teen problem, then we need to change course in a hurry.

A Second Opinion

The word *esteem* is used twenty-three times in Scripture, in four different tenses. It is interesting to note that it is never used in reference to loving or approving of oneself. However, it is used in reference to considering others. This was Paul's intended meaning when he said: "Let nothing be done through selfish ambition or conceit, but in lowliness of mind let each esteem others better than himself" (Philippians 2:3).

A biblical anthropological view of esteem conflicts with conventional wisdom. Although the goal is noble, we believe modern self-esteem proponents reverse the equation in insisting that feeling good is the precursor to doing good. According to that assumption, parents should build healthy self-esteem into their children before requiring anything of them. We take an approach that would liberate these parents. We believe that *doing good leads to feeling good.* Right behavior leads to right feelings, and the accumulation of right feelings leads to a healthy view of self.

We say that because we believe that doing right and consequently feeling right is rooted in a right relationship with God and His Word and in doing what is required of each of us. When a teen–or a child of any age–lives life in agreement with God's moral mandates, when his or her actions are aligned with God's relational precepts, that teen's conscience bears witness that his or her behavior is in keeping with the ultimate giver of life, Jesus Christ. Only when we are rightly aligned with God are we rightly aligned with self.

When you do the right thing, you feel approved, appreciated, virtuous–even when no one is looking. That's because your conscience, the silent witness of your soul, speaks to you either by affirming or accusing you regarding your actions. This is the basis for the statement, "Do something good; feel something real."

When you do a good deed or perform your civic duty or return to pay for that item you accidentally walked out of the store with, don't you feel good about yourself? Doing right leads to feeling right.

We speak with confidence regarding this subject. We have found that parents who place a greater emphasis on how a child feels than on how he acts experience a higher rate of teenage rebellion. It makes sense, though, doesn't it? If the highest good is a child who feels happy and pleased with himself, then anything that detracts from that feeling would be considered bad.

So, when Mom asks thirteen-year-old Chris to take out the trash, Chris lets her know that such a chore would make him feel neither happy nor pleased with himself. Mom feels guilty pressing anything on him that will wound his fragile self-esteem, so she relents. Or else she forces him to do it, which elicits great defiance from Chris. And why not, since he's come to believe that life is all about what makes him happy and that his parents' job is to see that he's kept that way?

What an irony! The very parents who work so hard to enhance their children's self-image actually end up creating the menaces to society they sought to eliminate. The more they feed the greed, the more the greed grows until they find they've raised greedy, selfish, ungrateful children who think the world ought to bend over backward to make them feel good.

In these families parent/teen conflict appears to rise proportionately to the emphasis given to early self-esteem training. More focus on good feelings equals more relational tension in the teen years.

Put your emphasis on leading your teen to do good because doing good leads to feeling good.

SYNDROMES AND DISORDERS

We hear about so many psychological syndromes and disorders: attachment syndrome, child depression, children's bipolar syndrome, ADD, ADHD, and oppositional behavior disorder. Today, when the psychologist is high priest, parents often feel that whatever strange behavior their teen exhibits must be the result of some neurosis or chemical imbalance.

There are children and teenagers who truly do struggle with legitimate mental and emotional disorders. You may, in fact, wish to have your teen evaluated. You can also find out about all of these maladies on the Internet and in your public library. But beware of looking for labels to justify misbehavior. We feel it is too much to lump every occurrence of antisocial behavior into the category of psychological disorders.

It's tempting to look to some kind of syndrome as the explanation for why our teenagers behave badly. It reassures us that we couldn't have done anything to prevent it. But defiance is fundamentally a heart issue. It certainly can be influenced by the strengths and weaknesses of personality and temperament and maybe even neurological deficiencies. But the bottom line is that it's a moral choice. If we choose to forget that, then even the most bizarre explanations become acceptable.

There is one common thread among most of these disorders: a lack of healthy sleep patterns. Before you take your child to a psychologist or therapist, and definitely before someone starts to prescribe a little white pill, maybe what you want to do is take him to someone who's involved in sleep research. Your family's physician should be able to make a recommendation.

Proper nutrition is another key to good emotional health. If your teen is subsisting on Twinkies and Taco Bell, that might be a clue for you. So before you take your teenager to a psychologist, make sure he is keeping good dietary habits and sleeping at least seven hours every night.

If you give good diet and healthy sleep a chance to work (a month or more) and you've seen no improvement, and you're sure your teen is not just lacking self-control or a sense of responsibility, then perhaps it is time to turn to someone who can give you an evaluation.

That doesn't necessarily mean going to a professional. Parents who have successfully guided their teens through situations like this are your best therapists. Before you spend any money, find someone in your church, or community who has already been where you are. Find out how they handled it and what happened as a result. You especially want to find families who have gone through it and have found tremendous success on the other end. These folks have experience, but they don't have a billing system.

If you do take your teen to a professional counselor, our recommendation is that you not take the first opinion that comes down the road. Be sure to get at least two opinions. Be very, very hesitant to put your teen on medication. Chemically subduing your teen is never preferable to solving the problem that's behind the behavior.

RELATIONAL TRAUMA

The breakdown of family harmony during the teen years can be attributed to many factors—mode and style of parenting, a weak marriage, drugs or alcohol abuse, parental manipulation, an overbearing mother, an absentee father—all will emotionally impact future family relationships. But the most painful relationship setback for children comes with divorce and, as often is the case, subsequent remarriage. As difficult as divorce can be on an adult, it is doubly difficult for children.

Today, many believe that divorce and remarriage make a negative impact on children and family relationships. They also contend, though, that children are emotionally resilient and can "bounce back" from the trauma of separated parents.

The rate of divorce is so high in the United States that now the family headed by original marriage partners is no longer the statistical norm. Some estimates put this group at slightly more than forty percent of our family population. This means a lot of families with teens are facing the added relationship issues of missing parents and/or the blending of two families. In tackling the impact this has on teen rebellion, there is no intention to condemn anyone's present circumstances. These remarks about divorce are intended to help single parents and blended-family parents understand the source of possible tensions.

From a teen's point of view, divorce violates the unspoken relationship covenant inherent in the family. With divorce comes a sense of betrayal. That betrayal is confirmed in remarriage. Remarriage dashes a child's hope of seeing the family reunited and leaves many children feeling emotionally abandoned. In the vast majority of cases, no child wants to see another man become dad or another woman become mom when the biological parent waits in the wings.

The way a child responds to the pain of divorce depends on his or her age. Younger children tend to respond by with-drawing from life, while older children may respond with anger, disappointment, and finally a rejection of relationships. If a child has had a strong attachment to the biological parents, the possibility of teenage stress increases with divorce and remarriage. If the relationship with the stepparent is poor, the probabilities for disaster are even higher.

On the positive side, blended families can avoid rebellion and relational rejection. The factors that make this possible are:

1. A strong relationship with the stepparent.
2. Confidence that the biological parent is loved.
3. Parents avoiding hypocrisy by living out the same values that they require of the teen.

Though both blended and single-parent families have built-in setbacks, God in His grace can help make the best out of every situation. This brings us to the end of our brief overview of how societal views have shaped your outlook on the teen years. Now let's take the next step toward restoring and reshaping your relationship with your teen.

SUMMARY

Teenagers do not usually rebel against authority; they rebel against relationships. They're not rebelling because it's their nature, because they're driven by hormones, or because they've got a disorder. They're rebelling because there is within every human a natural selfishness that makes us want to defy anyone or anything that's going to take away our self-governance.

Teenage rebellion is an unfortunate fact of life in America. But it doesn't have to happen in your home. Just because something is common doesn't mean it's inevitable. Statistically, divorce is common, too. However, most couples don't marry fully intending to divorce later. In the same way, you don't have to expect that growth from childhood to adulthood must result in a fractured relationship with your teen.

Questions for Review

1. Where does rebellion come from?

2. In the sentence which follows, fill in the missing words and explain the meaning of the sentence. "Hormones may affect _____ but not _____."

3. In healthy families, from what are teens seeking independence?

4. In unhealthy families, from what are teens seeking independence?

5. Do you agree that right behavior leads to right feelings? Why or why not?

The Power of Relationship

I. Introduction and Review

II. Moral Relational Approach

    A. It is a matter of fact that when you stop trying to improve your teen and start trying to improve your relationship with your teen, two things happen:

        1. You put the focus where it belongs on the _____.

        2. You start parenting by your _____ not your authority.

        By that statement, we are not asking you to abdicate your responsibility as a parent, nor are we suggesting that you let your teen do whatever he wishes or go wherever his passions lead him. But we are saying that adolescence is the time you best lead by your influence and strength of relationship.

    B. The Basis of the Moral Relational Approach

        Children mature physically and intellectually at differing rates. Yet in God's collective design of the four classes of maturity–legal, physical, intellectual, and moral–the one most responsive to human relationships is moral maturity, and it is also, when nurtured correctly, the first to blossom.

    C. The Key to Successful Teen Parenting

        The key to successful teen parenting is to have an _____ relationship with your teen even though he or she is not an adult physically or intellectually. This can only happen when your child reaches moral maturity. Moral maturity does not mean the child is all-knowing, but it does mean he knows and lives the "otherness" standard of Scripture.

D. Common Values

1. Whenever there is a breakdown in relationships, it's ultimately tied to a breakdown in _____.

2. Where there are no common values, there is no basis for family _____.

3. The general rule is this: The more each family member moves away from common values, the more strain is placed on all relationships.

E. The Benefits

1. Parents learn to lead by their _____.

2. It morally perfects _____.

3. Changes are for a _____.

4. It aids _____.

5. The world takes _____.

III. Principles for Starting Over
A. Tell God That You Want to Start _____.

B. Seek _____ for the Past.

C. Work on Your _____ Relationship.

D. Give Your Teen the _____ to Work on Your Weakness.

E. Become an _____.

F. Become a _____ of Your Teen.

G. Guard Your _____ and Your _____.

H. Encourage the Interdependent _____.

 1. Share at least one _____ together a day.

 2. _____ after dinner.

 3. Allow your teen to plan a _____ night.

 4. Let them participate in building family _____.

 5. Take _____ together.

I. Live your _____; don't preach it.

3

The Power of Relationship

W hen Mike and Stacy went to counseling with their daughter Connie, they thought the issues to be faced were school work, choice of friends, and broken family rules. After a few preliminary sessions of airing grievances, the counselor began to ask "why" questions. Time after time, Connie shrugged and answered, "I don't know." Mike and Stacy stepped in, suggesting possible reasons for Connie's behavior. "She grew so fast and always looked older than her age. She's not like our other daughter; Connie always had an independent streak."

In the middle of her parents speculation, Connie burst out, "What do you expect? Chrissy has always been your favorite. I was always the 'big girl,' the one who was to blame..."

Their daughter's revelation stunned Mike and Patty. They loved both girls. For the rest of the day, their minds ran reruns of the past. In bed that night, they talked. And as they thought back upon their behavior, the truth became clear. Somehow in their delight with their mild-tempered, golden-haired second daughter, they'd neglected their older one.

Unfortunately, this scenario is all to common. Each time a parent comes to us with such a story, we ask, "What came first?" Was Connie's continued defiance the cause of her poor relationship with her mom and dad? Or did an unintentional but nevertheless weakened relationship frustrate Connie to the point of noncompliance and rebellion?

Although rebellion is basic to man's nature and the root cause of many human conflicts, we have discovered that rebellion itself on the part of teens is not necessarily the root cause of all parent-teen crises. Many times it's not rules that teens rebel against but the authority who set the rules. We learned from observing teens in conflict with their parents, that when a teen is known and characterized by ongoing rebellion, the root problem is usually as much relational as it is moral.

Ouch! We know that statement can hurt, and we realize there may be many catalysts to rejecting a relationship. A physically or emotionally absent father, an overbearing mother, drugs, alcohol, physical and emotional abuse, not enough or too many rules, an under-controlled or over-controlled child, divorce, remarriage–all of these factors can produce stress. However, whatever the cause, the object of rejection is always the same–the relationship with parents. Why? Because that's where pain is felt. The striving for independence, the confused search for identity, the frightening influence of peers, the anger and battles of wills, the yelling, screaming, and threats–these are all symptoms but not the cause. For teens characterized by rebellion, they are conclusions not starting points. If you want to fix the problem, work on the relationship.

Our comments here are not intended to minimize the significance of sinful patterns of either teen or parent. However, we do want to speak directly to the power of right or wrong relationships, which often discourage or foster sinful conflict. Relationship building is the key to successful teen parenting, but it often takes time. There are no shortcuts to building new relationships or mending old ones. This takes effort, and there may be some pain involved.

Our society doesn't like pain. We want it to go away–now! In our efforts to get relief from our misery, too often we look for temporary solutions that mask the problem but will not fix it. Gary's older brother suffered almost daily from terrible migraine headaches. His only relief were two aspirin and the hope of sleep. Once during a routine dental checkup, the dentist noticed that one of his crooked incisors was placing abnormally high pressure on his upper jaw. A decision was made to remove the tooth for the benefit of the jaw. This turned out to be a right decision, although not for the reason it was made–after the tooth was removed, our brother's migraines disappeared. Months later the doctors concluded that a pressure-packed tooth had been the source of all his pain. Fixing the problem at the source relieved him of his misery.

Parents struggling with teens too often look for medicine that will mask the problems, rather than getting to the root cause. Often we want to fix the child, his youth group, his school, or a particular circumstance, but none of those "solutions" will fix the problem.

We are suggesting an alternative approach. We believe that when you stop trying to improve your teen by controlling him or his circumstances and instead focus on improving your relationship with your teen, two things happen. First, you put the focus where it belongs—on relationship. Second, you start to parent by your influence, rather than by your authority.

LEAD DON'T PUSH

When Mike and Stacy realized they'd neglected to build a strong relationship with Connie, they wept and asked God to forgive them. The next day they faced their daughters, unsure of how to fix the problem and how to remain the parents without repeating old mistakes. It was time for Mike and Stacy to make a new start with their teens, but they didn't know how. Perhaps you're asking the same question they asked: What does making a new start look like?

Let's begin with this first important truth: Seeking to rebuild parent-teen relationships does not mean abdicating your role or responsibilities as a parent, nor does it mean you should let your teen go wherever his or her passions lead. Adolescence is a time when your son or daughter is best served when you lead by your influence and strength of relationship, rather than by the power of your authority. The truth is, once your kids hit the teen years, your relationship—good or bad—is the greatest asset or liability you have.

When you have teenagers, it's important to lead rather than push. We can demonstrate this principle by using a common shoelace. Stretch one out on a flat surface in front of you. Make the end nearer you the "bottom" and the other end farther away the "top." Now, put your finger at the bottom of the shoelace and begin pushing. What happens? The shoelace begins to stack up in loops and tangles as you push, but it does not move forward. In fact, the more you push, the more it twists and turns, moving in every direction but the one in which you want it to go. Now take the other end of the shoe lace and begin pulling. What happens? You can lead the shoelace in any direction.

A values-based parenting approach teaches moms and dads how to lead in such a way that their teen desires to follow. Many parents wish to move their parent-teen relationship from where it is to where it should be, but they find resistance because they are pushing from the bottom rather than leading from the top. They are attempting to force change by the power of their authority, instead of leading by the power of their influence. We will discuss this further in chapter six.

ESTABLISHING MORAL COMMON GROUND

The belief that commonly held values leads to unity is not new. The apostle Paul encouraged the Philippians with these words: "Therefore if there is any consolation in Christ, if any comfort of love, if any fellowship of the Spirit, if any affection and mercy, fulfill my joy by being like-minded, having the same love being of one accord of one mind" (Philippians 2:1-2). Being like-minded, having the same love, and being of one accord–these attributes represent a noble goal for a Christian family. But how is such a goal attained? Only by establishing moral common ground.

In the family, just as in the Body of Christ, whenever there is a breakdown in relationships, that failure ultimately is tied to a breakdown in values. Because of that, you cannot start to build or rebuild strong relational bridges without a moral consensus. Bible-based, common values strengthen family ties. They are the glue that holds families together.

A moral consensus formed by common values also involves moral reciprocity. By this we mean that the moral rules for the teen are observed equally by the parents. When you remove the possibility of a double standard ("Do as I say, not as I do"), you remove the likelihood of hypocrisy. In its place will be relational security, confidence, believability, trustworthiness, partnership, family unity, and thus harmony.

This is an important concept to grasp because a principle factor to successful teen parenting is having an adult relationship with your teenage son or daughter, even though he or she isn't an adult physically, socially, or intellectually. This can only be achieved when your teen achieves moral consensus through moral maturity. When that happens, you will be leading more by influence and less by your authority.

WHO AM I? VALUES AND IDENTITY

Identity association is not a psychological invention developed in the halls of academia. It is a life-on-life dynamic found in all human relationships. It is a socializing process by which a person identifies with a group he or she is familiar with, attracted to, or feels empathy with. We derive our sense of belonging from our identity associations, and we give back to these affiliations varying degrees of allegiance.

Everyone has a potpourri of identity associations that provide a sense of belonging and allegiance. Some of these connections are casual and loosely tied while others are intimately linked with us. For example, every four years we identify with our Olympic athletes. By proxy, they compete for us. When they win, we win; when they lose, we lose. We also can identify with pain, hurt, and grief. Mothers and fathers who have lost a child to a drunk driver identify emotionally with members of MADD (Mothers Against Drunk Driving). If a parent has lost a baby to SIDS (Sudden Infant Death Syndrome), there is an identity link with the members of the SIDS Foundation. Closer to home, we identify with clubs, ethnic groups, professional trades, local sports teams, our church and denomination, our circle of friends, and of course, our own families.

Each of us has a number of identity associations to which we pledge a degree of allegiance and devotion and from which we receive an affirmation of belonging. So it is with teenagers and their identity associations.

Identity in Christ

To be a Christian is to be identified with Jesus Christ. In John 13:35, Jesus said, "By this all men will know that you are My disciples, if you have love for one another." Jesus established love as the identity for His disciples, setting His people apart from the world. The apostle Paul said believers are identified with Christ in His death, resurrection, ascension, and reign. A synonym for "identity" is the word union: "You in Me, and I in you" (John 14:20b). Used in this manner, identity is fundamental to unity.

Being part of a group identity does not take away from our individual uniqueness. In 1 Corinthians 12:20, the apostle Paul makes this point by saying, "But now indeed there are many members, yet one body." A person's identity does not take away from that person's individuality. Actually, each choice to identify with something or someone is an extension of individuality. In the Christian family, we are all individuals tied to a corporate identity in Christ.

The Defining Connection

Identity defines us by providing a set of socially understood reference points. A parish priest, for example, has a religious identity revealed in his clothing, speech, and lifestyle. The rock musician also is recognized by his clothing, speech, and lifestyle. They both have an identity that complements their values, and they both are identified by what they believe and how they act. People don't look at the rock musician and say, "Ah, there goes a religious man." Nor do they look at the priest and say, "There goes a pop singer."

With what or with whom we associate reveals who we are and what we believe. But there is more to it than just an outward association. Identity also promotes a sense of belonging. We feel more comfortable among like-minded people who uphold, justify, and support the existence of our values. In contrast, we feel isolated and sometimes threatened by groups that do not share our values. For this reason, we all tend to seek relationships with others who agree with our values. This is definitely true of teens.

Values either unify or divide people. Common values foster harmony and peace; opposing values can produce civil war. The more similar our values, the closer we tend to draw to people. The more values differ, the more people separate from each other. This holds true for families, parents, and teens, and it is the reason values-based parenting is highly successful. Parenting from a foundation of common values builds on the natural process of children to associate with their parents, gain a sense of belonging, and pledge their allegiance to the family.

In strong families, adolescence is not a time when teens seek a new identity. Rather, they attempt to validate the one they already have. Unless driven away by the influences described in this and earlier chapters, teens don't seek a primary identity apart from their families. There is no hidden, genetically controlled, instinctive dynamic that causes teens to automatically reject their parents and family in favor of peers—and that's good news for family relationships.

IDENTITY AND THE INTERDEPENDENT FAMILY

Among behavioral scientists, it is commonly accepted that teens are driven by a natural quest to find their own identity, and that they use peers to help establish and then validate what they believe. However, that's not true of teens who are members of an interdependent family.

Please take note of the prefix "inter" in the word interdependent. Like threads in a tapestry or two-by-fours in the frame of a house, each individual part supports the others in order to create the whole. The relationship of each thread or board to the others is mutual. In the same way, each member of the *interdependent* family is mutually dependent upon each other. Interdependency should not be confused with the popular counseling term *co-dependency*. When problems arise in interdependent relationships, the issue is confronted and each individual seeks to restore the whole. When problems arise in co-dependent relationships, fear and insecurity produce behavior that covers up the issue and functions around it.

Interdependent relationships provide satisfaction, protection, and security in the early years, and they serve as a barrier against intrusive values in the teen years. The interdependent family cultivates a sense of belonging that leads to allegiance to one another and allegiance to the core values of the family. Children grow with a "we-ism" attitude regarding their family rather than the selfish "me-ism" attitude that leads to lonely independence.

In contrast, the word *independent*, as used to describe the independent family structure, means to be free from influence, guidance, or the control of another. It also means to be unaffiliated, alienated, not committed to one another–in short, to be standing alone. These words are fairly descriptive of what takes place in the independent family structure.

On paper, most people would choose the interdependent family structure. Everyone wants to belong, to be supportive, and to be supported. But for the structure to work in real life, it means sacrifice. It means being there for one another. As parental heads of the home, it means the process begins with us.

There will always be better jobs, higher positions, advance classes, more convenient gyms, and greater opportunities for self growth and enrichment. These are all good, and it is hard to say no to them. But when parents no longer have time to fulfill their role as the primary moral influence over their children, the resulting vacuum will be filled with the voices of public institutions and their children's peers. The result can't help but be an increase in alienation, indifference, and independence on the part of the children.

You cannot expect family harmony when other people are socializing your kids with their values. The stronger the outside influences in the early years, the greater the potential division in the teen years.

Teens, Peers, and the Interdependent Family

Within the comfortable confines of the interdependent family, parents–not peers–usually have the greater influence. The very nature of progressive development reveals that teens choose their community identity–that is, their peer friends–only after their family identity is first established and then either accepted or rejected. If the family is accepted as the primary source of values and comfort, then the teen not only identifies with those values but makes friends from among those possessing similar values. This creates positive peer pressure.

When there is harmony between the core beliefs of parents and teens, then both seek similar values in other families and friends. That is why, ultimately, *peer pressure on a teen is only as strong as family identity is weak.*

The closer the values between parents and teen, the stronger the allegiance and the less likely that the teen will drift away from the parents. Once again, we need to realign thinking that has been skewed by popular belief: It isn't the power of peer pressure that tears adolescents from their parents, but a conflict in values that makes teens more vulnerable to peer pressure.

Please note that the strong family does not eliminate normal peer pressure as much as it develops healthy ways to deal with it. This is why it is wrong to blame peer pressure as the primary cause of drug use, crime, rebellion, sexual promiscuity, and the general breakdown of the family. Fundamentally, the problem is a matter of incompatible values.

Peers or the Independent Family?

There is a natural inclination for young children to identify with their families. There is good reason for this. For most children, the home environment is their greatest source of satisfaction, protection, and security. It isn't until they enter adolescence that peer pressure takes on maximum significance for children. During this period is also when prior parenting strengths and weaknesses are revealed.

Unlike the interdependent family, an independent family structure tends to promote incompatible values. When parents limit the fullness of their relationship in the formative years–birth through age twelve–by encouraging development of the independent family structure, the child upon reaching adolescence is more prone to seek an identity apart from his parents. He needs to fit somewhere. When the family is rejected and Christ is rejected, the teen is left with only his peer group to validate his beliefs.

To ensure peer acceptance, the teen learns that he must accept the group's interests and values. He cannot afford to be different because this would jeopardize his status within the group. To demonstrate his allegiance, he acts out his new association and conforms to the group's identity. This might be represented by choices in hairstyle, clothes, music, and the use of slang or foul language. Rejecting parents also becomes part of the teen's expression of group identity. Recovery is then made more difficult by the fact that teens react more readily to the approval and disapproval of their peers than to the approval and disapproval of their parents.

Passive Rebellion and Family Identity

More subtle than negative peer pressure, but just as destructive to parent-child relationships, is passive rebellion. Passive rebellion in teens is much like passive rebellion in young children. A child may be sitting down on the outside but not necessarily sitting down on the inside. Similarly, a teen can privately reject the family but publicly stay in touch with it–at arm's length. Passively rebellious teens are antagonistic to their parent's beliefs, but for any number of possible reasons, they are not ready to confront their parents with their own values.

Many teens wait until they are "out of the house" before revealing their true views, not feeling safe to express them while living at home. This is a dangerous situation. Like a person carrying a virus, you don't know if the sickness will spread, consume the host, or amount to nothing at all. These teens conform for conformity's sake until one day they simply are gone.

Passively rebellious teenagers reject their parents by moving into sports, clubs, or other group activities that provide a safe distance between them and their parents. They may even find their primary identity in a church youth group, rather than their own family.

Belonging to a youth group for some teens is a way of placating the parents by tolerating their values. Unfortunately, the problem becomes even more complex when youth ministries take on the resemblance of a para-family. A youth worker should not become the spiritual authority in a teen's life instead of parents. This betrays the family and undermines its leadership.

The message, "Your parents don't understand what you're going through, but we do," is divisive and does nothing to encourage family unity. Such statements actually justify teen antagonism by adding an air of legitimacy to any relational conflict. From a teen's perspective, "You don't understand me" serves both to justify and motivate further deterioration in ties to the parents' values.

Questions for Review

1. Explain the following statement: "Although rebellion is basic to man's nature and the root cause of many human conflicts, we have discovered that rebellion itself on the part of teens is not necessarily the root cause of all parent-teen crises."

2. What two things happen when parents stop trying to control a teen's circumstances and instead focus on improving their relationship?

   a.

   b.

3. Explain the following statement: Values either unify or divide people.

4. Think about why you agree or disagree with the following statement: "It is not the power of peer pressure that tears adolescents from their parents but a conflict in values that makes teens more vulnerable to peer pressure."

4

Starting Over with Credibility

When Phil and Bev started attending a *Reaching the Heart of Your Teen* class, their daughter Melody wanted nothing to do with it. She told her mom and dad, "This is just one more way you're trying to get me to do what you want."

After the first few workshops, Phil and Bev realized they'd been parenting in an authoritarian style. While talking with her husband, Bev said, "I guess this is why Melody thought the workshops were just another way to control her. But what now? How do we change? And even if we do, how will Melody ever believe the change? Everything we try is going to be suspect."

Bev wanted to know: How do we start over with credibility? This is a question that many parents ask. But before tackling the how, each parent must look at why he or she wants to start over.

Where is your relationship with your teen on the parent-teen continuum—filled with joy, filled with conflict, or somewhere in the middle? If your desire is to move closer to the positive end, consider whether you're truly asking, "Do I *wish* I could start over?" or "Am I *willing* to start over?"

Wish speaks to a fantasy of hope; willingness speaks to actual ability. As a Christian, you have the ability and the spiritual resources to start over with any relationship, and this certainly is true of the one between you and your child. Christ has made you complete (Colossians 2:10); He strengthens you and supplies your needs (Philippians 4:13, 19); and He has granted to you everything you need for life and godliness (2 Peter 1:3).

Christ has provided the tools for starting over, but are you willing and ready to use them? His expectations for us are high, so ours should be as well. Your goal is not just to turn out okay kids who don't do drugs, who avoid trouble with the law, and who as adults manage to support themselves. Those accomplishments are important but are relationally meaningless. The possibilities are so much greater. Your goal is to create a hunger within your child to love and serve each family member. Your goal is to have a family that is characterized by the positive aspects of the first twenty questions of our survey in chapter one. *The goal is relationship,* and it is never too late to start working on it. This is true whether your child is seven, seventeen, or twenty-seven.

Incidentally, the "you" and "your" in the previous sentences refers to parents as a team, as well as to individual parents. For optimal results, the two of you must engage in the cycle of change, willing to work toward a new relationship with your teen. But if you're a single parent or your spouse has an unwilling heart, don't lower your goal. Timothy became an outstanding godly man because his mother, Lois, developed a close, moral-based relationship with him.

START WITH YOURSELF

Practically speaking, where should you begin? How do you go about mending relationship bridges which have been badly damaged? How do you change old habits of parenting this late in the game? How can you bring about positive moral changes and not just outward ones that are nothing more than your teens placating you, or you them?

The first step is often the most difficult of the entire journey. Perhaps you made attempts in the past to reform your teen. Maybe you've tried discipline, grounding, rewards, the hard sell, the soft sell, the church youth group, sports, family counseling–all with no improvement. Your efforts have resulted only in pain. You feel worried, helpless, hopeless, humiliated, and guilty. When the realization finally hits that you can't control your teen despite all your efforts, you feel utterly defeated. Your relationship hurts, and you're discouraged. Can you, with God's help, really move from a negative to a positive relationship at this point?

We are convinced that when you make a sincere and sustained effort to change yourself first, other positive changes will occur. But it must start with you, the parent. You must be the initiator. Work to increase your influence. Become credible in the eyes of your teen. Do whatever is required to demonstrate your desire to change the status quo.

Learning how to manage your teen is secondary to learning how to lead your teen by your moral influence. That means you must take the lead in this quest and not give up. We'll deal with behavior management in later chapters, but for now, the goal is to build your credibility so you can lead by your influence, rather than by "laying down the law."

The rest of this chapter contains suggestions for helping you get started. Applying them now can help minimize further erosion, while effecting a positive change in your relationship with your teen.

TELL GOD YOU WANT TO START OVER

Your heavenly Father knows everything there is to know about your family. He knows your pain, fears, and anxious moments. He delights when you, His child, ask Him for divine guidance. James, the brother of our Lord, reminds us of a simple truth: "You do not have because you do not ask" (James 4:2b). Starting over with our children, regardless of their age, means approaching the Lord and inviting Him into our lives to reveal, expose, and change us.

In Psalms 139:23 David pleaded with God, "Search me, O God, and know my heart; try me, and know my anxieties; and see if there is any wicked way in me, and lead me in the way everlasting" (Psalms 139:23-24). He wanted God to lay bare the sinful condition of his heart and to lead him up the path of righteousness.

Join David in his plea. Ask the Lord to reveal those things in your life that hurt Him. Then confess your sin–both unintentional and intentional. Either way, your sins and weaknesses must be brought to God. We all need a heavenly cleansing before we tackle our earthly problems. We must receive the Father's forgiveness and then His wisdom to parent effectively.

No parent purposely sets out to do an ineffective job of raising his or her children. But many are misguided by the philosophies of this world and end up doing just that. There is forgiveness and hope. God understands your despair. Encourage yourself with these words: "If you say, 'Surely we did not know this,' does not He who weighs the hearts consider it? He who keeps your soul, does He not know it? And will He not render to each man according to his deeds?" (Proverbs 24:12). Tell God you're ready to start over.

SEEK FORGIVENESS

When God answers our prayers and exposes our sin, it must not stop there if our sin has touched other lives. The only way to get beyond our past is to seek forgiveness. Please note that asking for forgiveness doesn't mean saying, "I'm sorry." That phrase should be reserved for unintentional mistakes. For example, if you unintentionally step on your teen's model airplane and break the wing off, you apologize by saying "I'm sorry." You may even pay to replace the model, but no malice was intended.

Seeking forgiveness, on the other hand, is different. We seek forgiveness when we knowingly do wrong–by deed, inactivity, or speech. To say "I'm sorry" is to acknowledge a mistake; to ask for forgiveness is to acknowledge wrong motives of the heart. This distinction is very important. When we intentionally offend another, we have an obligation to seek forgiveness by asking for it, rather than declaring how sorry we feel. To simply say "I'm sorry" or "I apologize" is not enough. Sorrow is subjective and can range from little to great. Forgiveness is objective and has no middle ground–it's absolute. That means it is either sought after or it's not. There is no such thing as partial or conditional forgiveness.

Our friend Allen seems to be in a perpetual state of war with his youngest daughter Rebecca. The suggestion of starting over by seeking forgiveness was not easy for him to accept. It wasn't a case of him rejecting the biblical injunction to forgive; he simply feared that admitting wrong would cause him to lose the little control he still had over her.

It is humbling and often extremely hard to seek out a teen who's hurt you and seek his or her forgiveness. But it is humility that begins to build credibility. It is humility that opens the door to leading by influence. It is humility that does not expect a preconceived response from your son or daughter. To admit to being wrong does not detract from a parent's authority or leadership. On the contrary, it teaches integrity. It worked for Allen.

Seeking forgiveness for past mistakes should not be limited to you and your teen, but should extend to you and your spouse. It's easy to shift blame, to point a finger at someone and mumble, "We wouldn't have these problems if you listened to me and didn't give in as much." Or to say, "If you were around more, things would be different."

Each parent has contributed to the present state of affairs, both positively and negatively. Each makes deposits toward healthy family advancements, and each contributes his or her share of mistakes. But blaming each other for the negative and staying silent about the positive is not going to help solve family problems. However, forgiving each other will (Matthew 6:14; Luke 6:35-38).

Ask the Lord to give you the courage to confess to each other your weaknesses and your hidden patterns of fear. We encourage single parents to find a friend who can hold them accountable and encourage them along the way.

Confession and forgiveness can help break sinful patterns set in motion long ago. They afford an opportunity to start fresh. Do this for the sake of your relationships and for the sake of your children, remembering that your children will always be your children. Only death marks the ultimate deadline for reconciliation.

MARRIAGE FIRST

If you're together in a marriage, work on your husband-wife relationship, not just on your role as a mom or dad. Some people wonder, "What does our marriage have to do with our parent-teen relationship?" Answer? Everything. Young children have an innate desire to know mom and dad love each other. That desire never leaves, not even when the child moves into adolescence and adulthood. If the husband-wife relationship is not visibly healthy, why should a teen emotionally invest in the family? If the two people leading the family can't get along, family renewal can hardly be expected.

Roger and Kim's thirteen-year-old son Neil demonstrated this truism. As a youth, Neil was out of control and troublesome. It was at a point of desperation that Roger and Kim sought help through a *Growing Kids God's Way* parenting class. But the challenge was to find someone to stay with Neil during their class. Because he could not be trusted to stay home alone and no one volunteered for the job, they brought their son to the church and sat him in back of the auditorium while they sat down front each week watching the video presentation.

In session three, the topic centered on the husband-wife relationship and the inherent need for children to know concretely that mom and dad love each other. That week's homework assignment directed parents to take fifteen minutes a day, when dad or mom comes home from work, and sit on the couch as a couple and talk. Such a simple task repeated daily, we explained, demonstrates to children mom and dad's friendship and togetherness.

After his parents had neglected their assignment for three days, Neil, in a moment of crisis, charged his parents with not loving him. "Why can't you give me what I really need? Why can't the two of you just sit on the couch and show me that you love each other. You haven't done anything the man on the video said to do."

Apparently Neil was doing more than sitting in the back of the auditorium reading his biker magazine. Out of his own desperation, he was listening to every word of the presentation, hoping for change. It never occurred to Roger and Kim before that moment that even Neil understood this self-evident truth: Good marriages is the breeding ground for good parenting. More than anything else they could do or say, their son wanted to know, "Do you love each other, Mom and Dad?" From that moment on, Neil was a changed teen because his parents started to really love him by demonstrating their love for each other.

Every step taken to improve the marriage is a step toward strengthening the parent-child relationship regardless of the age of the child. As you eliminate conflict in marriage, you eliminate conflict in parenting. There is a definite correlation between strong marriages and successful parenting. The marriage relationship is the stage upon which the performance of trust is acted out before an audience of watchful eyes and hearts. The way your children see you loving and nurturing each other highly influences your believability.

There is a widespread myth that kids don't like to see their parents "act mushy." This is simply not true. Children–even teens–thrive on the demonstration of love between parents. They want the confidence that dad and mom are tremendously in love with each other. A beautiful marriage makes family life attractive.

A father can be wonderfully active in the life of his children. He can take them hiking, fishing, skating, and camping. He can help them with their homework and drive them to every school function available. But he will undermine the security his good efforts should produce if he is not putting the same time and energy into loving his wife. The unconscious question triggered by a neglected mom is, What will keep dad from some day neglecting me?

In the same way, a mom can spend twenty-four hours a day with her children, being loving and sacrificial all the while. But her efforts have limited impact with her kids if she fails to demonstrate an unfailing love for her husband.

How much trust can a teen have in parents who won't take time to appreciate and be with each other? How much trust can a son or daughter have in a dad or mom who continually speaks harshly to his or her spouse, or demonstrates a lack of patience, or manipulates the marital relationship? How can the child of parents in conflict be confident of their love for him or her while questioning their love for each other? Love between parents is basic to healthy family relationships.

LET THEM HELP YOU GROW

The idea of asking your teen to help you work on your personal weak areas may seem risky or frightening. Please try it, because we know it is an effective way to help get healthy parent-teen relations on track.

Your teen has lived with you for thirteen to nineteen years, and believe me, he or she already knows your weaknesses. Being imperfect is easy for parents. Accepting your imperfection is harder. Inviting your teen to point out your weaknesses can be downright painful, yet it's necessary for both your child and for you.

One characteristic of strong families is the freedom granted each member to lovingly confront one another when necessary. Sensitivity and wisdom must be applied if such interaction is to be effective. Both parties must be open to learning. And the individual being confronted must be willing to listen. The purpose of this confrontation is not to condemn but to strengthen; it is not to incite conflict but to provoke one another to love and good works (Hebrews 10:24). The Holy Spirit provided the New Testament Church with a procedure permitting a believer to go to another in the Body of Christ to encourage and admonish him. This same strategy works for strengthening family relationships: "If a man is overtaken in any trespass, you who are spiritual restore such a one in a spirit of gentleness, considering yourself lest you also be tempted" (Galatians 6:1). Notice the guidelines. You are to employ a spirit of gentleness and are to remain aware of the power of sin in your own life.

We practiced this principle in our own family. As parents, we knew we had parenting blind spots—wrong perspectives, lack of patience, occasional over-confidence in our decisions or too little confidence in our children's. We knew our teens saw all of our frailties. They knew our strengths and weaknesses. Realizing that no one desired that we know the truth more than our own children did, we invited and even encouraged them to help us become better human beings. In doing so, we communicated to our children that we trusted them. We trusted their motives, and we trusted their discernment. That expression of trust spoke volumes to our kids. We didn't just let them "have at it," but we set up some guidelines governing the privilege. Remember, although the following rules are written for teens confronting their parents, the same principles of respect can guide parents in confronting their teens.

1. Teens cannot verbally assault their parents. They must speak honestly and honorably at all times.
2. Both teens and parents must be in agreement on the particular weakness or weaknesses to be worked on.

3. Teens must come with a desire to help, not accuse.
4. Teens must be in control of their own attitudes when making an observation or accusation.
5. Struggling teens must want to start over. Their willingness to do so validates their desire to have a relationship with mom and dad.

There are some advantages to giving your teens the freedom to work on your weaknesses. First, it fosters within you a healthy vulnerability. The popular notion is that vulnerability denotes weakness, but we're using the term to indicate strength. One of the keys to unlocking the door to the human heart is healthy vulnerability. To be vulnerable is to be open to the healthy censure or criticism of morally mature members of the family.

Vulnerability helps keep the inner person in check. It permits another person to hold up a mirror to our face so we can see who we really are and who we are becoming. When we hold the mirror to our own face, we tend to look only at our good side. Our teens are very good at showing us all sides. Teens detest hypocrisy in their parents; our vulnerability and openness to their input helps prevent it.

A second advantage develops when your teen makes an investment in the parent-teen relationship. What you invest in, you care about. This truth hit home when a relative persuaded us to invest in a European company doing business in the United States. We bought their stock at $18 a share. Within a month our stock jumped to $21 a share. Over the next several months, we watched our stock go up and down and back up again.

Getting involved in the stock market gave us a new appreciation for the word investment. Every day we found ourselves looking at the Dow Jones averages. My attention turned from what we did initially with our investment, to what we wanted to do with it, to what we felt we must do. We guarded and nurtured our shares. We remained focused on the returns. The more growth we saw in our investment, the more committed we became. If our returns began to diminish, our investment received renewed attention.

The same is true with relationship investment. Giving our teens the freedom to work on our weaknesses allows them an opportunity to invest relationally and emotionally in us as well. There is one clear truth about human nature and the nature of investment: People tend not to walk away from an investment that costs a great deal. Personal investment gives us a reason to stick around—to nurture, watch, and add to our stock.

Your teen will do that with you. But first you must give him or her a healthy prospect of real rewards for his investment–you. Are you willing to be vulnerable and open to investment? How is your relational portfolio? Without those two attributes, your teen has no pathway to your heart and no hope for a healthy return.

BECOME AN ENCOURAGER

There is a big difference between uttering an occasional encouraging remark and being an encouraging parent. Real encouragement flows out of a relationship. It's more than a word now and then; it's your very presence, smile, and expression that communicates encouragement.

It is easy to encourage a friend; it's much harder to encourage someone with whom you are in conflict. Yet encouragement means more to a weakened relationship than to a strong one, especially when it comes from a former foe. Continuous and honest encouragement communicates a willingness to change the status quo–a desire to move forward the relationship.

How about writing a little note? This is a practical way to communicate encouragement. Think back to your childhood. Did you ever receive a handwritten note from your dad or mom–something beyond the usual Christmas and birthday-card greetings–something simple, encouraging, and ending with the precious words, "I love you"? If so, you know how precious such a gift can be. If you did not, it's likely that you can imagine how such a gift could have made you feel.

It doesn't take much to occasionally put a note in your teen's lunch or school book–maybe a thought or two on last night's ball game or the walk you took together. The time it takes to write a twenty-word note is probably thirty seconds, but the impact on your child can last a lifetime. The older the child, the more he or she needs to hear encouraging words from you.

One step up from note writing is letter writing. Letter writing provides an excellent forum to communicate what really is in your heart. The very nature of expressing yourself with pen and ink allows you to select your words carefully, to qualify your thoughts, and to communicate your intent. Conveying your thoughts on paper is especially helpful when you know face-to-face communication often fails. Take time to express your concerns, struggles, and frustrations, and share the hopes, desires, and joys of your relationship.

No matter what style of communication you choose–words, notes, letters, or another form–take your teen's need for encouragement seriously. Don't wait for warning signs to tell you how much your teen needs you. On the surface, it may seem as though nothing in particular is claiming your child's attention. On the other hand, he or she may be dealing with issues that on the surface seem trivial. But to a teen in the midst of a trial, struggles that remain unspoken or are barely hinted at can be serious business. Many times parents underestimate a child's plea of urgency. Problems which appear trivial to us may seem insurmountable to them.

Listen for cues and realize there will be some matters of major importance couched in insignificant sounding statements. By listening carefully, you may be able to pick up on a serious problem with a friend, teacher, or foe, or you may get wind of a problem involving peer pressure and your child. They need your help and encouragement, whether or not they will admit that to you.

BECOME A STUDENT OF YOUR TEEN

What makes your teen tick? What is his particular giftedness? What are his favorite pastimes? Does he like computers, sports, classical music, or the hum of a high-powered engine? If you haven't already, you must become a student of your teen. Learn to ask open-ended questions that require a thoughtful response. Rather than asking, "How is school going?" to which your child can reply "Fine," try digging a little deeper. "What's the hardest/best part about your new math class?" "What teachers this year do you think will be the easiest to get along with?" Such information is too valuable to waste.

Tremendous insights can be gained by observing how teens live their lives. Teens, like adults, carry on an existence in three worlds: public, personal, and private. Their public world includes much of their time away from home such as that spent at school, work, and attending public events. Much closer to home is their personal world. Here teens live among family members, close friends, and relatives. It is within the secret chambers of the heart that we all live in our private world.

Your teen resides in all three worlds and becoming a student of your teen means gaining access to all three. We found that growing to really know our own daughters required nothing less. Regular visits to each of their three worlds helped us maintain in our mind a composite sketch of who they were and who they were becoming.

We learned a great deal about our daughter Amy–about her sense of competition, fairness, and her attitudes about victory and defeat–by going to her junior and senior high school basketball games. How she lived her convictions on the court, in the locker room, and at practice added to our understanding of her complexity. Her public world provided a different window of observation from the ones through which we saw her most often. It gave us, as her father and mother, a more complete picture of who she was.

The same was true of our daughter Jennifer. She had a knack for handling money, finances, and investment. She knew more about the bond market at seventeen than either of us will probably ever know. Whenever we had a major family financial decision to make, Jennifer was always there helping us work through the issues. When you become a student of your teen, you have opportunities to borrow from their strengths. This, in turn, affirms them and strengthens your relationship with them.

In starting over with your teen, discover in which world your son or daughter spends most of his or her time. Does your son spend more time away from the family than in it? Is your daughter the type who keeps to herself, secretly finding security in her private world? The key to understanding your teen's public and personal worlds is to be in them when appropriate.

Sporting events, club activities, recitals, and school functions can give you access to your child's public world, but entry into their private world comes by invitation only. Quality time spent with the teen there can open the window to the private places of the child's heart. In our home, these special moments were planned as often as not. When we really wanted to hear from the kids or when they wanted to hear from us, we went out to lunch together to a neutral meeting place where we wouldn't be interrupted. Once there, we as parents listened with both our heads and our hearts.

Outside activities also provided opportunities for communication. Going for a walk, to a ball game, out for a morning stroll through the mall, fishing, boating, or on a long bike ride together put us in close proximity, which is necessary for heart-to-heart sharing. Don't rely upon chance meeting times to hear from your children. Plan for those times, and make those opportunities happen.

ENCOURAGE INTERDEPENDENCE

Each member of a family must learn to communicate honestly and listen attentively. Are you willing to provide opportunities for your children to talk and then to listen to them? Below are five practical suggestions to help cultivate that all-important alliance.

Share at Least One Meal Together as a Family Each Day

To live with a teen is to live in the fast track. Because time demands can loosen family ties and put serious strain on already weak ones, extra effort must be put into keeping the family together. That's why we committed ourselves to regrouping each night at mealtime. That sometimes meant our schedules had to change, and sometimes theirs did, but we were committed to having one meal together each day—to relax, talk, recharge our emotional batteries, find out what was going on in each other's lives, and to enjoy our growing friendship with our teenagers.

Research has shown that teens who eat with their family are better adjusted than those who do not. A study of 500 adolescents at the Cincinnati Children's Hospital Medical Center found that those who ate with their families at least five times a week were less likely to be depressed or use drugs than teens who ate with their parents only three times a week. The former kids also had better relationships with their peers and were motivated in school.

With all that is going on in their lives—school, sports, youth group, club activities, socials, friends, and employment—scheduling family time when everyone can be there is a challenge, but it is one that must be met.

Read After Dinner

Reading together is becoming a lost family art, yet it is one of the most pleasant activities that can be shared between parents and children of all ages. After dinner each night, before the dishes were cleared from the table, Anne Marie led our family in a story time. It was one of our greatest pastimes. George Mueller, D. L. Moody, Hudson Taylor... one chapter a night allowed us to walk with the great men and women of the Christian faith.

Reading together after dinner did more than add to our minds. It was during times like these that we really gave our children what they needed—a sense of family identity built upon the memories of our togetherness. If you're starting over, reading after a meal is one good place to begin.

Allow Your Teens to Plan a Family Night

Some people think having leisure-time activities with your children is a luxury. It is not a luxury; it's an absolute necessity. Family night helps keep your work and play in perspective. We planned a family night once a week. It was a time when we separated ourselves from work and school and came together for family fun. Family night afforded us an informal setting for relaxing with family members who didn't care how our hair looked or what we were wearing.

We eventually added a little twist to our weekly family fun night. Long before our children reached their teen years, they took ownership for every other family night. They did a little budget and planned the evening. We played board and card games, had indoor picnics, or feasted on pizza and fondue and watched a favorite video classic.

What are the benefits derived from family night? Your children are not just taking ownership of a family night every other week; they are actually taking ownership of your family. It is their investment into the fun portion of other family members' lives. It adds another good reason for them to stick around. Plan family nights. This ensures that your children don't end up with your leftover time.

Let Them Participate in Building Family Memories

Not only can you encourage your teen to plan a family night, but you can take the next step and encourage him or her to help you plan the next family vacation. Whether it be a short weekend camping trip with your church Sunday school or a week-long event away from home, planning and participating adds a positive, memory-building dimension for your teen. The more healthy the memories, the closer you grow as an interdependent family.

Building memories with your children means more than taking them places and doing fun things with them. It requires that they become participants in all aspects of the activity. This truth was realized by friends of ours many years ago. For years they left the February cold of northern New England to spend two weeks in warm Florida. Each year our friends returned home discouraged by their children's constant complaints and lack of appreciation for all that the parents felt they had done.

Then one year someone suggested they let their kids help plan the next family trip. That included letting them help decide the travel route, make some of the scheduling decisions, and select some of the special events they would attend along the way. It made all the difference in the world. What made the difference? The children became participants in the vacation instead of spectators. What was the overall benefit? The work that went into planning and scheduling, the anticipation of seeing those plans realized, and the sense of ownership all factored into building lasting memories for each member of that family.

Take Walks Together

If your response to this is, "Yeah, right–three hundred years ago," give it a chance. It may surprise you that this simple suggestion might get accepted. We found that taking walks with our children–one at a time–brought about conversations we otherwise would not have had. There is something about a twenty-minute walk that causes people to reflect, open up, and share their hearts. Those moments of reflection often led to very personal and private conversations with our girls.

Walking with our children gave them access to us and gave us access to them. They exposed their inner thoughts, fears, doubts, and hopes. Sometimes they just needed to talk, which meant those walks were good times for Anne Marie and me just to listen. We knew our listening served a purpose; it provided a sounding board to help our children sort things out.

Dining, reading, planning, playing, and walking together. This is just a partial list of the activities we have enjoyed together as a family. Make your own list. See if you can come up with ten options. What are some of the favorite activities of your individual family members? Pick out one or two that you can try doing together this week. Now do them!

LIVE YOUR CHRISTIANITY

One last credibility builder is your own personal integrity. Healthy families govern themselves from a clear set of values. For the Christian, this set of values is biblical–at least they are supposed to be.

Probably one of the most destructive forces in parenting a teen is hypocrisy. Parental hypocrisy occurs when mom and dad exempt themselves from the set of values they require their children to uphold. This double standard happens when you tell your kids church is important, but then you tear down the service or members while driving home. It happens when you tell your kids never to steal, but you don't return a clerk's accidental overpayment of change. Hypocrisy breeds contempt, leading to relationship breakdown.

For our family, the Bible was the final authority. The Word of God was the umpire settling all our disputes. Only biblical ethics provide the safeguards needed to prevent parents from becoming hypocrites because only a biblical approach calls both parent and child to accountability. The moral rules that apply to our children also apply to us.

Solomon said it was the little foxes that destroyed the vineyard (Song of Solomon 2:15b). The little acts of hypocrisy that may have gone undetected in the early years stand out as beacons during the teen years. Parental hypocrisy dismembers the family. If you are starting over or just desiring to improve your parent-teen relationship, don't just preach your Christianity; live it.

BEGIN TODAY

Are you willing to start over? If so, there are a few things you should consider as you begin the process of reparenting and relationship-building. First, gather everyone together for a family conference. Reveal the mistakes you made in the past, and then seek your children's forgiveness. Next, discuss what God requires of parents and children. Don't skip over His expectations for you! If the issue is obedience, what does God require in that area? If it is respect, what does His Word say about that? Share how your family has been functioning contrary to biblical ethics and establish a common ground from which all family members will work in the future. Explain the next course of action that all of you will be undertaking.

Finally, after answering all their questions, join together in prayer asking the Lord to give you and your teen the wisdom to do that which is right with a fresh new beginning. The key to starting over is consistency. When you start over as a family, your teens will scrutinize you and your spouse from a distance to see if there are any changes. Do everything you can to make your efforts count. By God's grace, you can and will achieve a new beginning with your teen.

Questions for Review

1. Are you a good encourager? Is your marriage strong? Review this chapter's credibility builders. What do you believe is your strongest point? Your weakest? What can you do to improve?

2. Explain the following statement: "Learning how to manage your teen is secondary to learning how to lead your teen by your moral influence."

3. What is easier for you to say, "I'm sorry" or "Will you please forgive me?" Why? What would you like to do differently after reading this chapter?

4. Name two advantages of giving your teens the freedom to work on your weaknesses.
    a.

    b.

5. Biblical ethics provide safeguards that help prevent parental hypocrisy. Why is that so?

The Many Ways of Love

I. Introduction and Review

II. The command to Love
    A. It Is Required by God.   John 13:35

    B. It Is a Frustrating Command

        1. For some, love is an action void of _____.

        2. For others, love is a feeling with no regard for _____.

    C. The Heavenly Example

        1. Christ loved in action, which led him to Calvary's _____.

        2. Christ demonstrated His love in feelings at the _____ of His friend Lazarus.

        3. The basis of love:

III. Learning How to Say "I Love You"

We all recognize that one of deepest human needs we have is the need to feel loved. God made us emotional creatures with the capacity to feel love and equally important to communicate love to others. But many parents and teens do not know how to say "I love you" in action, so that the person they are directing their love towards actually feels loved. We do love our children, even those with whom we are in conflict. Our love has become frustrated. That is usually because we have not learned how to say "I love you" in the emotional language of the other person.

A. Love is Communicated through _____ Languages.

B. Five Languages of Love

    1. _____ of encouragement

    2. Acts of _____

    3. _____ -giving

    4. _____ time

    5. Physical _____ and closeness

C. Communication Exercise

From the five love languages (words of encouragement, gift giving, acts of service, quality time, and physical touch and closeness) list and rank, from priority to the least, the love languages of your spouse or your parent. This is not a list of what you think your mate or parent would like, but what he or she actually speaks.

Next, rank yourself starting with your primary love language. Third, rank the children in your family. Once completed, compare lists and see how well you know each other. (Please take note of the fact that the Love Language test in your workbook is much more comprehensive than this basic introductory exercise.)

Exercise one: Rank your mate, your children and yourself. Primary language = #1. The least = #5

Name   Name
----

1.   1.

2.   2.

3.   3.

4.   4.

5.   5.

Name   Name
----

1.   1.

2.   2.

3.   3.

4.   4.

5.   5.

5

The Many Ways of Love

In our family we joke about "ums." "UMS" is a little-known condition usually found in individuals on days when everything goes wrong–from getting cut off on the freeway to getting called in for a "little talk" with the boss. UMS stands for "Ugly Mood Syndrome," and on this particular day Gary had a bad case of it. Anne Marie and Jennifer weren't around when he got home, but eighteen-year-old Amy was out in the garage working on a project. When her father found her, she grinned and said, "Hi, Dad. You're home."

Normally, this innocent greeting would get a similar one in return but not when suffering from UMS. "Amy, what are these boxes doing in the garage? How many times have I told you girls I want them kept on the shelves? And there is Styrofoam everywhere. I want this mess cleaned up right now! Is that my good hammer?"

What happened next is still hard to believe. It took a lot of courage and even more love. Amy put down her project and walked over to Gary. Then she put her arms around him and said, "You must have had a hard day, Dad. You need a hug."

LOVE BEYOND THREE WORDS
It wasn't easy for Amy to love her father that day, and sometimes it isn't easy for parents to love their teens. But love is not an option for Christians. It is a command. In John 13:34 Jesus said, "A new commandment I give to you, that you love one another; as I have loved you, that you also love one another."

Jesus Christ is an example of purest love–the best example there has ever been. He left heaven's splendor to come to earth and die for mankind (Philippians 2:6-8). As He loved, we are to love. It's as simple and as complex as that.

Knowing how to love as Jesus loves is vital to showing our teens and others the truth of Christ. In John 13:35 Jesus said, "By this all will know that you are My disciples, if you have love for one another." Love is the badge that identifies us as disciples of Jesus Christ. God wants us to love each other so the world will know we belong to Him, and the place to learn about love is in the Christian home.

TWO SIDED LOVE

Love has two sides: giving and receiving. Giving love is the action side; receiving love is the feeling side. For some people, love is an action void of feeling; they just do "love." For others, it is a feeling void of action. There is talk of "love," but no demonstration of it. Not having a balance in love is what ultimately makes the process of loving frustrating.

Actions and feelings, in the context of love, do not need to conflict with each other. Jesus was not emotionless. He loved in action and with feeling. His love in action led Him to die for us. His feelings of love were demonstrated with tears at the death of His friend Lazarus (John 11:35). Actions and feelings are part of the equation of love, and like other biblical truths both are often violated.

We all recognize that one of the deepest emotional desires we have is to feel loved. God made us to be both rational and emotional creatures. We have the capacity to feel loved and, equally important, the ability to choose to demonstrate it. But loving others can be frustrating if we're not sure our actions are interpreted as love. The question we must somehow find the answer to is this: How can I demonstrate love in action so that the person I am directing it toward actually senses love?

We know that parents naturally love their children. We also know they can become frustrated in that love. They try many different ways of saying "I love you," but sometimes there is no evidence that the child feels or appreciates that love. It may seem that the harder parents try, the less the child values the effort.

Many parents have a wrong view of how to express love to their teen. They sometimes believe saying "I love you" means giving their teens anything they want whenever they want it. Appropriate gift-giving can be a valid expression of affection for a child. But extravagant giving on demand does not demonstrate love–certainly not biblical love. Such expressions will never lead teenagers to feel good about themselves or feel loved by their parents.

We need to learn how to say "I love you" in ways that get our message into the hearts of our children, filling their emotional needs. Authentic expressions will cause your teen to say the same right back to you.

LOVE AS AN EMOTIONAL LANGUAGE

Love is expressed through emotional languages. A love language is the ability to express love and concern to another person in the primary emotional language of the other person. Gary better understood this need to express love in the other person's primary love language on his first visit to the former Soviet Union.

While walking through the famous Red Square, a typical once-an-hour crowd assembled to watch the changing of the guard at Lenin's tomb. Gary joined them. The people who were gathered there spoke their native tongue–Russian. Since it wasn't Gary's native language, nor did he know how to speak it, the words held no meaning to him. The sound receded to a hum in his ears. As the replacement guards started their march toward the tomb, Gary suddenly heard off to his left, "Hey, Larry! Come over here. You can get a great picture!" Instantly his head turned.

Gary tuned in right away because someone was speaking his native tongue, English. Even if someone had spoken in Spanish, he would have paid attention. It isn't his native language, but having lived in Southern California where that language is often spoken, he would have identified it–not as quickly as English, but he would have identified it since Spanish is his second strongest language. French is his third. He doesn't register its meaning as quickly and misses some words, but he has some understanding of it. The point is this: the languages we are most familiar with are the ones we readily tune in.

What happens with spoken languages also happens with emotional languages. We may speak our primary emotional language, but it often comes across to other people as an unknown tongue. We say "I love you" in one language, while they say it in another. As a result, our efforts to demonstrate love are frustrated. When this happens within our families, we are tempted to walk away emotionally from our children and our mates, thinking no one cares about our attempts to love. To avoid this frustration, we need to learn the five basic languages of love and discover which one is the "native tongue" of each family member.

Love Language One: Encouraging Words

The apostle Paul identified the power of love when he told the Corinthians that love edifies or "builds up" (1 Corinthians 8:1). One way of expressing love is by building up others through verbal encouragement. "You're such a compassionate person. I could learn a lot from you." "The flower garden looks beautiful. You must have worked on it all day." Or, "That dress really looks terrific on you." But these words will only touch the heart if they are sincere. Flattery is not encouragement. Taking the time to verbally pat someone on the back is a way of saying "I love you." For some, there is no greater way to express love than with words of legitimate praise and recognition.

Love Language Two: Acts of Service

The apostle John encouraged Christians to love with action and in truth (1 John 3:18). Sincere acts of service is another way of communicating love. This means doing something special for another person, something you know he or she will appreciate. Normally, this is something outside the realm of everyday routine. For a husband, this might be putting gas in his wife's car on Sunday night so she doesn't have to worry about filling the tank that week. Or maybe he will express his love by fixing the leaky faucet or by making the shelves his wife wants in the closet.

When a husband comes home from work, believing the patio needs sweeping and finding it already done by his wife, he has a heightened appreciation for his wife on the basis of that act of love–especially if "Acts of Service" is his primary love language. Because he didn't expect it, the act means more to him. He is aware that she did it because she knew how much he would appreciate it. Whenever you do something for another person beyond the normal course of events, you are saying "I love you" in action.

Love Language Three: Gift-Giving

The greatest gift of love the world has ever known is Jesus Christ, who gave Himself for His Church (Ephesians 5:25). Gift-giving is a third way of saying "I love you." Even simple or no-cost gestures can pack great meaning because of what they represent. Impromptu gift-giving (unlike giving gifts on occasions such as birthdays or holidays when they are expected) sends the message, "When we are apart, you are on my mind. This gift is a token reflecting my thoughts of you." The message goes even deeper into the heart when the gift is the other person's favorite color or something they collect. This type of gift adds, "I'm paying attention to you and noting what you care about." A modest gift is a meaningful token that can say to a discouraged heart, "I love you."

Love Language Four: Quality Time

The gospel record provides insights into the quality time Jesus had with His heavenly Father and with the men He discipled. Although His goal was to train His disciples for ministry service, He recognized that they needed to spend personal time with Him. That time with the Master brought their thinking into conformity with His.

We can begin to define quality time by stating what it is not. It is not sitting on the couch reading the newspaper or watching television together. Quality time requires that you invest yourself in the other person—your child or spouse. It includes listening carefully and giving an appropriate response to what is being said. It involves two people who are actively participating in the conversation and going beyond the fact level of communication. The time spent at this may only be ten minutes, but for the person whose love language is quality time, those ten minutes are precious.

Love Language Five: Physical Touch and Closeness

Think of what it must have been like to be one of the children described in Mark 10:13-16. Jesus gathered them in His strong arms and blessed them, using the children and their love as an object lesson for His disciples.

Within the context of a marriage relationship, some spouses assume that because they enjoy lovemaking, their primary love language must be "Physical Touch." This is not the case. The language of physical touch and closeness is more far-reaching than that. It is a special way of saying "I love you." Holding hands, putting your arm around your spouse's or child's shoulder, warm hugs, or just standing close to each other can telegraph a special love message.

Another example of this love language is this: A husband is working in the garden and his wife sits down nearby with a book and begins to read. She could have read the book anywhere in the house, but she chose to be close to her husband. This, too, transmits a message of love. Some couples enjoy being near each other even when silence prevails. Simply knowing the other person is nearby can confirm a partner's affection and care.

WHAT LANGUAGE DO YOU SPEAK?

Of the five love languages, one is your primary language. One of those modes of expression means more to you than the other four, and another one means the least to you. Your primary love language is the one you most enjoy having expressed to you and the one you tend to "speak" to others. However, learning how best to say "I love you" in the primary language of your spouse or child often means stretching beyond what you prefer to what each of them prefers.

Scenario One

Bill and Sally had a good Christian marriage, yet the full sensation of love was missing. They knew they loved each other but also felt frustrated in communicating it. It turned out that Bill's primary love language was physical touch and closeness. He spoke that language and felt loved when it was spoken to him. The language that meant the least to him was words of encouragement. In contrast, encouraging words was Sally's primary language, and the last on her list was physical touch and closeness.

This couple loved each other but didn't know how to communicate their love in a common language. Bill often would ask his wife, "How about a hug?" In turn, Sally wished that Bill would write her more notes and letters like he had when they were dating. She wanted to hear words of encouragement, while he desired physical touch and closeness. Sally would do many special things in the front yard, hoping that when Bill walked through the door he would say, "The rose garden looks beautiful. Thank you for your efforts." Bill did walk by the garden and appreciate her work, but rarely would he communicate his pleasure in her primary language.

At a seminar addressing the five love languages, Bill and Sally learned that every day each of us chooses whether or not to communicate love. When they understood that basic truth, each of them chose to love the other in his or her primary language. Bill now says "I love you" with words of encouragement. He leaves notes around the house or calls his wife during the day. He now chooses to communicate love verbally. Sally has chosen new ways to express her love to Bill too. She now speaks his language of physical touch and closeness. She initiates hand-holding, giving hugs, and standing close to Bill during social gatherings. As a result of them both choosing to love in accordance with the other's primary language, the fullness of love has returned to their marriage.

Scenario Two

Dave's primary love language is acts of service; Ruth's is quality time. After work, Dave would come through the door, embrace his wife, and receive an invitation to sit and talk before dinner. Dave would agree and suggest that she make some coffee while he changed his clothes. Ruth would then go to the kitchen to prepare a snack; then she would sit down and wait for her husband.

After a few minutes, she would say, "Honey, the coffee is ready. Are you coming?" He'd respond, "I'll be right there, dear. There was some laundry on the bed, and I'm putting it away." A few more minutes would go by, and she would call out again, "Coffee is getting cold." This time he would answer, "Coming, dear! I was hanging up my tie and noticed that the light bulb had burned out. I'm going to change it for you."

After a few more minutes passed, she would hear him in the kitchen and once again ask, only now with an edge in her voice, "Are you coming now, dear?" She'd hear back, "I'm just throwing the old light bulb away." When Dave finally got to the couch, Ruth was getting up. "Just forget it. I'm sure you have something else to do!" Dave would be bewildered. What did he do? *I try to do so much to help her.* The problem Ruth experienced was not that her husband didn't love her. He demonstrated his love through acts of service. But as wonderful as that is, he was not speaking her emotional love language.

Scenario Three

For twenty-five years Betty begrudgingly accepted the many gifts her husband Mike brought for her. Time and time again she'd think, *This is frivolous. I don't need this.* Occasionally, she would catch a glimpse of hurt in Mike's face but would dismiss it. After all, it was just a gift.

Later, Betty learned about the five love languages and instantly recognized her husband's. She wept, realizing for the first time that she was rejecting her husband's expressions of love to her. What compounded her sorrow was learning that gift-giving was on the bottom of her list of love languages and that she rarely spoke that language to him—except at holidays. How discouraging it is to say, "I love you," only to be rejected time and time again!

Betty learned the hard way that we must not only learn to speak the primary love language of our partner but must also learn to receive graciously all the expressions of love that come our way from those around us.

Scenario Four

Gift-giving was last on the list of love languages for Kevin's mother and father but it was first on his. His parents noticed that on each trip to the store, he consistently asked for money to buy something. For years, they interpreted his requests as an abnormal materialistic hang-up. They worked extra hard to break him of that trait but with a frustrating lack of success.

When Kevin's parents learned about love languages, they realized that their son's primary love language was gift-giving. Equipped with a better understanding of their son, they tried a different approach. They started to bring home little gifts: a pack of gum, some pencils, a fancy eraser–nothing expensive, just a little something to say "I love you." That practice virtually eliminated his asking for things in the store. Mom and dad learned to say "I love you" in a language their son could readily understand. If they hadn't, Kevin's teen years could have centered on a parent-teen relationship void of feeling loved.

WHAT LANGUAGE DOES YOUR TEEN SPEAK?

As our last scenario indicates, it is just as important to learn your teen's primary love language as it is to learn your spouse's. Gift-giving is the primary love language of our younger daughter. Many times we entered our home to hear Jennifer say, "I made you a surprise." Whether she baked a cake, pie, or cookies, she was saying "I love you" through gift-giving. In this case, she didn't give us something she had purchased but a gift she had made herself as an act of love. In turn, we would do the same for her, often giving Jennifer little gifts. For example, we would buy a ribbon for her hair, causing her face to light up with a bright smile because that little gesture confirmed in her heart our love for her.

Quality time is our older daughter's primary language. When we realized that, one of the two of us would take Amy out for a leisurely lunch whenever possible. By this, she knew we were saying "I love you" in a language she could easily understand. Moments of quality time happened throughout the week too, but when we sat down at lunch and gave her undivided attention, love was confirmed in her heart.

Without some insight into primary love languages, it is easy for parents to misdiagnose a child's behavior and misjudge motives. This can result in frustrated parents and confused teens. We made the mistake ourselves.

After a weekend trip, we brought home stuffed bears for our children. When we gave one to Jennifer, she smooched and hugged us, saying, "Mom, Dad, thank you! This is wonderful. I love this little bear!"

Later, we couldn't help commenting to each other, "That girl has such a thankful heart." When we gave Amy her bear, she responded, "This is nice. Can I talk to you?" "Come on, Amy," we pleaded. "Don't you want to arrange your new bear among all the others in your room?" After attempting to convince her of how wonderful the gift was, we turned to one another and concluded that Amy was not as thankful as Jennifer.

That was the wrong diagnosis! Amy was as thankful as Jennifer; we just misinterpreted her actions. They meant something different than what we thought. Not understanding the dynamics of communicating love can be costly to a relationship. It is easy to misdiagnose a child's motives based on how we interpret his or her actions. That is why knowing a child's language of love is critical.

BIBLICAL LOVE

By now some of you might be wondering where 1 Corinthians 13 and other biblical teachings about love fit into the "languages" picture. God's call to love as He loved is what makes us choose to speak the other person's love language. Biblical love looks outward not inward, yet at the same time it satisfies all the inner needs.

In order for your teenagers to acknowledge the preciousness of others, they need to have learned a sense of love from you. Having a confirmed sense of love is not the basis for right behavior, but it does clear the way for a more comprehensive, proper love of others. One of the best ways to change a heart is to love that person when he or she is most unloving.

When biblical love is in the life of a teen, he or she will not be held back by the shackles of self-love, self-interest, and self-protection. The same is true of the parent. In one sense of needing to feel loved, we all remain children. That is why the family is so important. It should be a secure haven from which love flows. The ongoing demonstration of love between mom and dad should spill over to the children. Always remember: Everyday we choose to love or not to love.

When we express love rightly in the context of the family, it makes it easier for each member to say "I love you" to those outside the family. When we love with a biblical love, we rightly represent God to the world.

Questions for Review

Do you know each family member's love language? Here is an exercise that we want you and your teens to try. Within each group, rate the sentence 1 – 5 according to what would make you feel most appreciated and loved by your spouse (or your parents or your teen). The number 5 represents what you most appreciate; number 1 in contrast is what you least appreciate in each group. (No individual grouping can have a number repeated twice.) Please note that some questions distinguish between male and female. Answer those appropriately, according to your gender and position in the family.

Group One

A ___   Your spouse/teenager/parent says: "You really did a great job on that. appreciate it."

B ___   Your spouse/teenager/parent unexpectedly does something in or around the house or your room that you appreciate.

C ___   Your spouse/teenager/parent brings you home a surprise treat from the store.

D ___   Your spouse/teenager/parent invites you to go on a leisurely walk just to chat.

E ___   Your spouse/teenager/parent makes a point to embrace and kiss you before leaving the house.

Group Two

A ___   Your spouse/teenager/parent tells you how much he or she appreciates you.

B ___   Your spouse/teenager/parent (male) volunteers to do the dishes and encourages you to relax. Your spouse/teenager/parent (female) volunteers to wash your car and encourages you to relax.

C ___   Your spouse/teenager/parent (male) brings you flowers just because he cares. Your spouse/teenager/parent (female) brings you home a special food treat from the local bakery.

D ___   Your spouse/teenager/parent invites you to sit down and talk about your day.

E ___   Your spouse/teenager/parent gives you a hug even when he or she is just passing by room to room.

Group Three

A ___   Your spouse/teenager/parent during a party shares about a recent success you had.

B ___   Your spouse/teenager/parent cleans out your car.

C ___   Your spouse/teenager/parent surprises you with an unexpected gift.

D ___   Your spouse/teenager/parent surprises you with a special afternoon trip.

E ___   Your spouse holds your hand as you walk through the mall or your teenager/parent stands by your side with an arm around your shoulder at a public event.

Group Four

A ___   Your spouse/teenager/parent praises you about one of your special qualities.

B ___   Your spouse/teenager/parent brings you breakfast in bed.

C ___   Your spouse/teenager/parent surprises you with a membership to something you always wanted.

D ___   Your spouse/teenager/parent plans a special night out for the two of you.

E ___   Your spouse/teenager/parent will personally drive you to an event instead of you having to go on the old crowded bus with the team.

Group Five

A ___   Your spouse/teenager/parent tells you how much his or her friends appreciate you.

B ___   Your spouse/teenager/parent takes the time to fill out the long complicated applications that you had hoped to get to this evening.

C ___   Your spouse/teenager/parent sends you something special through the mail.

D ___   Your spouse/teenager/parent kidnaps you for lunch and takes you to your favorite restaurant.

E ___   Your spouse/teenager/parent gives you a massage.

Score Sheet

(Transfer your scores from your test questions to this scoring profile.)

	Encouraging Words	Acts of Service	Gift-Giving	Quality Time	Physical Touch
Group 1	A____	B____	C____	D____	E____
Group 2	A____	B____	C____	D____	E____
Group 3	A____	B____	C____	D____	E____
Group 4	A____	B____	C____	D____	E____
Group 5	A____	B____	C____	D____	E____
Totals	A____	B____	C____	D____	E____

Compare your score with your spouse/teenager/parent. Write down from the primary to the least of the love languages of each family member.

1._____

2._____

3._____

4._____

5._____

Start to speak each other's primary love language.

From Authority to Influence

I. Introduction and Review

II. Understanding Authority and Submission

    A. Obedience versus Submission

    B. Freedom versus Responsibility

III. The Moral Reason Why

    A. Moral Action versus Moral Thought

    B. Providing the Practical Why

    C. Starting Point of Moral Training

IV. Understanding the Importance of Context

    A. Why Context?

    B. Avoiding Legalism

6

From Authority to Influence

We start this chapter with two truths. The first is that parenting is a process leading to maturity. Who among us was mature enough to have children *before* our children came? It seems that children are not just a blessing that results from marriage–they are part of the process that produces two mature beings: mom and dad. The second truth is that nothing of value comes quickly. Whether you're just starting to build a strong family or beginning to repair a weakened one, the process takes time.

If we have learned two things from counseling with parents at war with their teens, they are: It is natural to try to control something that is out of control, and especially for parents, change can be frightening. Yet, we are asking you to face this fear–to put aside your authority and begin to work toward leading your teen by the strenght of your relational influence.

Scarry prospect? As one father shared, "If I give up my authority, my kid will run all over me." Another mom explained, "Lead by my influence? I don't have any influence over my daughter. She does what she pleases. I can't stop her." These are very real concerns. If they are legitimate, then it's time to consider another alternative. Apparently controlling by your authority hasn't worked for you. Something else can.

MORE OR LESS?
Now that your child is in the teen years, it's time to ask yourself: Am I using more or less of my authority to bring about moral conformity? Consider carefully your answer to this question. While many parents feel tempted to exert greater control during the middle and teen years, we want to stress that *you must begin to rely less upon the power of your authority*. As your preteen approaches

adolescence, the need for your parental rule should decline in direct proportion to his or her increased rate of moral self-rule.

The teen years are a potentially confusing time not just for your child but also for you as a parent. Changes are occurring within your son or daughter, yet you're not entirely sure what is happening. Like many moms and dads, you may fear the unknown. You may feel anxious about what lies ahead. This apprehension can spark a desire to increase your control. At times you may feel that the best way to manage the future is to bring in the boundaries to more fully control your teen.

Or, perhaps you may go to the other extreme and completely surrender, saying: "There's nothing I can do. During the teen years my child is going to do whatever he wants to do." As the teen years draw near, you find yourself pulled into the despair felt by so many parents in our society.

Nowhere is there greater confusion than around the stormy topic of parental control and use of authority. It seems the unnecessary controversy has replaced common sense. The permissive parent looks at the authoritarian parent and says: "I don't want to be like that mother and father. They're too strict!" Meanwhile, the authoritarian parent looks at the permissive household and says, "I don't want my children acting like that. Those kids are out of control!" The permissive parent who controls too little and the authoritarian parent who controls too much both deprive their children of basic skills necessary for healthy adolescence. Too often these kids hit the teen years either under-directed or under-motivated.

You have another choice. You don't have to increase your control at this stage of the game, nor do you have to back away from your authority. As you approach your child's teen years, you can transition from relying upon the power of your authority to tapping into the power of your relational influence. This is the one great transition every parent must make.

THE AUTHORITY EXCHANGE

Mankind has always struggled with authority. But authority is absolutely essential because law and order for the family and society are dependent on its proper administration. In the Christian family, the Bible not only provides the basis of all authority but also the ethics that govern how it should be used. Like the character of love (1 Corinthians 13:5-7), biblical authority is full of integrity, gentle, consistent, and gracious, and it is not presumptuous, proud, unkind, or unfair.

Biblical authority is motivated by love and used only when needed. Its purpose is to guide by encouragement and restraint.

Certainly parental authority can be taken to extremes (and obviously at times it is). Too much authority leads to totalitarianism, while too little leads to injustice and social chaos. This is true for nations; it is also true for families.

As we've already mentioned, the teens years are a time of great change not just for your child but for you as a parent. Perhaps the greatest transition you will experience is that of learning to use less of your authority and more of your influence to motivate your child. Here is a basic truism we want you to remember: *When children are young, parents should led by the power of their authority. When children move into the preteen and teen years parents should lead by the strength of their relational influence. Between the two points the need for parental authority should decline as your child begins to exercise moral self-control.* By the time your child hits adolescence, you will have exchanged rule-centered leadership for principle-centered leadership. Here is what it looks like diagramed.

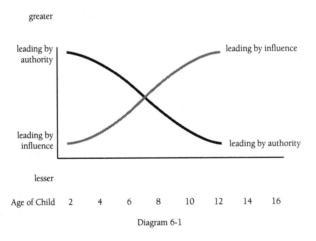

Diagram 6-1

To illustrate this point further we can borrow an example from a live class session. Please note that, while the lead child in this story is only ten years old, the principles apply equally to a teenager. This illustration starts with Carla, a mother of three, who after a parenting class approached Anne Marie with a question. She listened attentively to Anne Marie's response, reluctantly agreed to try what she had suggested, and went home. When she returned to class the next week, she shared enthusiastically the following results. Here is a transcript of her conversation as she spoke to an audience of her peers.

I have three girls. Whitney is ten, Brenda is seven, and Carissa is four. Like most parents I have a real fear about this next phase of parenting, especially with my ten-year-old. I had a little talk with Anne Marie last week about an incident involving Whitney and sharing.

I explained to Anne Marie that Whitney had a bag of popcorn and Brenda asked for some. Whitney said no. This really bothered me because my seven-year-old is so generous with her sister, almost to a fault. So I intervened and told Whitney that she had to share. She finally did.

When I thought through the incident, I knew I hadn't done the right thing, but I didn't know what I did wrong. So I asked Anne Marie what she thought I should do. I was surprised when she told me to think about not always inter-vening with my authority and forcing my kids to share with each other. This was a frightening prospect for me. I said to Anne Marie, "How long will I be doing this? What if this goes on forever?" Anne Marie assured me it would not and asked that I try this for several weeks and see what happens.

In God's perfect timing, the next day another incident took place. Whitney had some mints and Brenda asked for some. Whitney said "no" and Brenda imme-diately looked to me for help. I told Brenda, "If Whitney doesn't want to share with you that's fine. God wants sharing to come from our hearts or it is not real sharing." Brenda protested for a few moments, and I went about my business.

A little later my ten-year-old came to me and asked, "It's okay if I don't share, Mom? Is that what you said?" I said, "Yes, that's what I said." Whitney left, but in that very moment I could see something had changed in her heart. Five minutes later she was generously sharing all her mints with Brenda.

The next day, all I heard from the two girls was: "Can I borrow your this? Can I play with your that?" I was shocked. Non-coercive sharing was foreign to my children. It was foreign to me.

So I called my ten-year-old aside and asked, "Whitney, why are you so will-ing to share all of a sudden?" And this is what she told me: "Mom, this is how I always felt, but you never let me do it without telling me I had to. I wanted to show you how I feel, but you never let me do it without making me. I want to show you that I know how to make a wise decision and do the things you and daddy taught us."

I went home last week and gave up trying to control all the outcomes by using my authority. In a very marginal way, I started to use the power of my influence by speaking truth in love with my kids. I can tell you in one week's time, Whitney has become a different child—mostly because she has a different mom. And while I am still using my authority with Brenda, I can see why I need less and less of it to guide Whitney.

There is one more thing I learned through this experience. In the past when I tried to control all outcomes I was actually robbing my kids of the joy of doing right. I can see that now. At Whitney's age, there is no joy in doing right when the actions required are always tied to my authority."

Can you relate to Carla's story? We sure can. We remember similar situations that occurred during our preteen and teen parenting days. Please note what Carla did *not* do: she did not abandon her God-given authority. What she *did* do was start the process of giving up her power to control all outcomes. Now she works to bring about right outcomes by leading through her influence.

Consider for a moment how you once controlled everything about your child's day. During his infancy, you determined when your child ate, slept, stayed awake, had a bath, played on the blanket, or went for a stroller ride.

Such tight supervision is absolutely necessary during the early years, since a child does not know how to regulate his own day for his own good. But as children grow, they become more responsible. When your child was five, you no longer controlled or directed his day to the same extent as you did years earlier. At five, children can come and go from the back yard, pick out their own board games, play with their hamster, or go to their rooms and play with a puzzle. Because they continually demonstrate responsible behavior in these areas, parental policing is no longer necessary. Our point is this: Although parental authority is still a considerable influence in a five-year-old's life, it is not as sweeping in its control as it was a few years earlier.

The same holds true of a ten-year-old. With the increase of self-rule there is a direct decrease in the amount of parental policing required. It's not that mom and dad's authority is no longer valid, but that the need for outside control is diminishing. Gradually, parental control is being replaced by parental influence. External motivations that once governed the child's life are replaced by internal beliefs that rule from the heart. Moral maturity emancipates the child, allowing him to direct his own behavior in harmony with family values.

At this point we want to make clear that we are not suggesting that you eliminate house or family rules. Your teen is still accountable to you. There are community tasks and responsibilities that need to be maintained. In other words, your child still needs to take out the trash, make his own bed, clean up after himself, be home at a reasonable hour, and yes, comply with parental instruction. However, the basic tasks of life should take on new meaning—a moral one in response to a relationship to the family. No longer are they simply a response to an impersonal set of rules reinforced by coercive authority.

You may feel a bit awkward as you begin the exchange of authority for influence. However, this change is absolutely necessary for a successful transition to occur. Take just a moment to consider: *Where am I right now in the process of authority exchange?* Are you using more or less of it?

MORE THAN JUST WORDS

Just as in the Body of Christ, whenever there is a breakdown in relationships between family members, the failure ultimately is tied to a breakdown in values. This is why you cannot start to build relational bridges without first having a common source of values. Common values, when Bible-based, are what strengthen family ties. They are the glue that holds families together.

Having common values means that the moral rules children live by are also observed by mom and dad. When you remove the possibility of a double standard ("Do as I say, not as I do") you remove the likelihood of hypocrisy. In its place will be relational security, confidence, believability, and trustworthiness.

By adolescence, your child should have begun to acquire a moral code to which he or she voluntarily adheres with increasing frequency. The more your preteen voluntarily yields to that code the less parental authority is needed—but equally so, the more parental *example* is required.

A child who has been taught that it is wrong to lie and who attempts to be honest will lose all motivation to live honestly if he sees that his parents do not do so. When a parent violates the truth of a conversation or describes a dubious business deal, he or she loses all credibility in the eyes of the preteen.

Kids are extremely sharp; they notice when there is a disparity between our words and actions. Naturally, they conclude: "What's good enough for Mom and Dad is good enough for me." The inconsistency between values preached and values lived will always force a greater need for parental policing than would have been necessary if parents themselves were greater examples of the virtues they tried to instill.

By the time your child reaches moral maturity–between the ages of thirteen and fifteen–your parental authority should be nearly invisible. Though you still exercise it, more often your teen's behavior is controlled by voluntary self-rule. Conforming voluntary self-rule means only one thing: relational unity and a unified family is a wonderful place to be.

Questions for Review

1. Explain the major premise of this chapter.

2. What is the differnce between leading by parental influence and leading by relationship?

3. Explain your understanding of the following statement taken from Carla's story: "At Whitney's age, there is no joy in doing right when the actions required are always tied to my authority."

7

Principles of Moral Training

Today morality comes in all shapes and sizes. "If it feels good, do it" says one bumper sticker. Even in Christian homes values differ. There's a tendency to end up with a potluck of morality—some from the previous generation, some from Bible teachers, some from authors, and some from society's subtle influence.

What's so wrong with taking a potluck approach? Why do parents need to test their values against the standard of God's Word? First and foremost, Christian values reflect the person of Christ. Such values trigger a child's consciousness of God and eternity. The natural world is seen, heard, felt, smelled, and tasted. But the supernatural world is revealed through quiet and unseen things like Holy Spirit revelation, faith, and the values that reflect both.

Second, because biblical values are others-oriented, a child trained in them is bathed in otherness sensitivity—a prerequisite for healthy and enduring relationships. Jesus was other-oriented and set the ethical standard for the "one another" of Scripture. Biblical values produce the moral mandate of Scripture that requires a love-God, love-your-neighbor sensitivity (Mark 12:28-31). We should not base our conduct toward others based on how valuable they are to us, nor on any value found in our humanity, but on how beloved they are to God (Romans 8:35-39).

Third, biblical values promote unity. Moral relativism segregates society into cultural subgroups, but biblical values are socially, racially, ethnically, economically, and educationally blind (Galatians 3:28; Colossians 3:11; James 2:1-10). Without God's morality, behavior is governed by personal preference.

MORE THAN THE MIND

Godly values instilled into a person's life will make a positive difference whether that person acknowledges God or not. But it is the hope and focus of Christian parents to raise a morally responsible person who realizes Jesus Christ belongs in his or her life. Only then does moral training go beyond the mind and into the heart. Only then do God's values go beyond being a positive life influence to being a way of life.

Does your son or daughter know Jesus Christ? Pray, pray, pray that he or she does, but don't let your desire for such a relationship blind you to what may not be the case. Unless your teen's life reflects a profession of faith made as a young child, leave room for the possibility that your teen might not know the Savior. Moral common ground must be built on what the parent and teen truly share in common, not on what parents want to have in common. Biblical values are not a substitute for a life with Christ, but they represent the standard of conduct that conforms to God's moral laws.

Jesus Christ wants your child's heart. But it is hard to trust God with it. Somehow we think, *If I just share the right verse. If I just get him into the right youth group. If I just...* Parent your children by trusting God, not fearing circumstances. Pray and then pray some more. Your goal, then, in parenting is to share the need for Jesus Christ, to instill godly/moral values, and to build on this moral common ground. You aim for your child's heart but realize only God can reach it.

WHAT NOT TO DO

Dos and don'ts are both a part of moral training, but too often Christian families concentrate on the don'ts. Parents can get more occupied with suppressing wayward behavior in their teens than in elevating good. That is, when teaching moral precepts, we often tell our kids what is wrong and what not to do, rather than what is right and what to do. Compounding the problem is the preeminence we place on training during periods of conflict. Think about it for a moment—most parents tend to teach in moments of conflict when they tell their children what *not* to do, rather than in moments of non-conflict when they can direct their children in what *to* do.

Negative moral training leaves a void that can cause serious moral compromise in the future. Because so much emphasis is placed on what to avoid and too little on what to do, the way to moral goodness is left undefined for the child. As a result, only the restraining half is internalized and not the half defining right-living. Certainly, suppressing the waywardness of a teenager's behavior is important, but when this is done in the absence of elevating good, the parent ultimately ends up distorting what "good" really means.

For example, a child taught to be sensitive to how people feel in situations has a stronger basis for future behavior than one merely taught to control his anger. Teaching our kids to do deeds of kindness is greater than teaching them not to be unkind. Restraining evil has to be balanced by elevating good. Moral restraint and moral assertiveness are two sides of the same coin and both are needed in the training process.

Parents are in a position of great influence when it comes to helping their children internalize godly values. But how is that goal best achieved? Here are three considerations.

IT BEGINS WITH MOM AND DAD

When it comes to developing a moral common ground, Moses had a whopper of a task. Hundreds of thousands of Israelites left Egypt with values turned and twisted by three hundred years of idols and false gods. In Deuteronomy 6:4-7, Moses told his people, "Hear, O Israel: The LORD is our God, the LORD is one! You shall love the LORD your God with all your heart, with all your soul, and with all your strength. And these words which I command you today shall be in your heart. You shall teach them diligently to your children, and shall talk of them when you sit in your house, when you walk by the way, when you lie down, and when you rise up."

From these four verses we can glean three principles of moral instruction. First, unlike the beliefs of the Egyptians, there is only one God to please, Jehovah God. He is an absolute God, and His commandments are consistent with His character. God is morally perfect and all biblical values are an extension of His character. Potluck morality is out!

Second, the starting point of moral training begins with the parents. Before you diligently teach your children, Moses said: "These words... shall be in your hearts." If the principles of moral conduct are not resident in your own heart, you cannot pass them on to your children. It's a mistake to think moral training is the duty of the Sunday school, day school, or Christian school teacher. It is not! By intent or neglect, parents are the greatest moral influence on their children. Thus the words of Moses speak to the heart of the matter–the parents' heart.

Third, moral training is to take place during the normal activities of the day. "You… shall talk of them when you sit in your house, when you walk by the way, when you lie down, and when you rise up." By implication, moral truth is best communicated in periods of non-conflict. That doesn't mean we will not teach at times of correction, but it does mean a healthy dose of moral enlightenment should take place throughout the day and in moments of non-conflict when the child is not in a position to have to defend his or her actions.

The charge to parents from this passage is to know the God of moral truth, live His moral truth, and from that experience teach your children that truth.

THE HOWS AND WHYS

It is not enough to teach your children how to *act* morally; you must also teach them how to *think* morally. To accomplish that goal, you need to think in accordance with biblical values. Moral thought is a prerequisite to the process of raising a morally responsible child.

A major reason children do not internalize values is because moral instruction too often lacks a moral reason. By that we mean mothers and fathers often tell their children what to do but don't tell them why they should do it. That distinction must be emphasized because knowing how to do right and knowing why to do right are definitely two different things. The first speaks to moral action, while the second speaks to moral principle.

Many children know how to apply moral law, but not as many know the why behind it. When they go to church, children are told how to act; when they go to school, they are told to obey; when they go to grandma's house, they are told how to behave. Thus, a greater emphasis is placed on the how-tos than the why-fors. As a result, some children reach adulthood appearing to be moral on the outside but lacking morality on the inside.

When we say parents should provide a "why" in their instructions, we don't mean parents are obliged to provide an explanation for every decision or instruction on demand. There will be times when the explanation "because Mommy said so" is enough. This is especially true in the toddler years. But from three years of age and up, parental instruction should become more characterized by the inclusion of the moral and practical reasons why they should do what we tell them.

The Moral Why

After morning services some of the kids from the junior high group began to ride their bikes on the church patio in between churchgoers. When Ryan handed his Bible off to his dad and headed toward his bike, his father stopped him and asked about Ryan's intentions. "I'm going to ride around the church with the guys," Ryan told him. His dad responded with, "Ryan, I'm going to ask you not to do that." Then he did what is characteristic of proper biblical training: He gave his son the moral reason why.

Ryan's father explained that riding on the church patio was not appropriate because of the presence of others. He pointed out mothers with their babies, senior citizens coming and going (some with canes), folks in wheelchairs, and the people chatting with hot coffee in their hands. He helped Ryan see the potential danger and explained why riding his bike in such a circumstance was not morally acceptable. This time, dad governed Ryan's behavior; next time Ryan can do so on his own because the principle has been placed in his heart.

To further illustrate the importance of giving our kids the moral reason behind our instructions and restrictions, let's extend this hypothetical situation a bit further. Let's assume that Ryan's father denied him the opportunity to ride with his friends but never gave the moral reason why. We have found that when "no" is given without explanation, kids view the rule as applying only for today. Next week when Ryan's friends once again invite him to ride around the patio, Ryan will have no good reason not to ride–because no moral reason was placed in his heart. If there is no principle to stir the heart, the heart will not be stirred. Children who do all the right things without knowing why they are right are moral robots. They often respond to situations and circumstances correctly, but not from any guiding principles of the heart. Getting the heart involved in life choices is an invaluable asset in adolescence. It is a prerequisite in order for you to lead your teens by your influence.

PREVENTING LEGALISM

In developing common moral ground, one thing to guard against is crossing into legalism. A legalistic approach to parenting is very dangerous, especially in the teen years. It leaves in its wake a frustrated teen. Legalism creates prohibitions by elevating the rule over the principle. The legalist sees all decisions in life as either black or white, immoral or moral. He or she acknowledges no heart or motive areas. No room is made for individual strengths and weaknesses. The legalist tends to demand that the consciences of every believer be identical.

We have all heard the exhortation, "Let's keep things in context." The most notable aspect of a legalist is that he or she rejects context. Responding to the context of a situation does not mean we suspend biblical laws or principles but that we apply them in the most appropriate way. If someone gossiped about you, it does not allow you to slander.

Considering context guards against legalism and helps a person determine how to confront the problem. Take Andrea's case. Her dad told her, "Honey, I don't want you to park the car on the street. Keep it in the driveway." He expected to be obeyed. But when the neighbor started to spraypaint his house and some drifted toward the parked car, Andrea moved it to the street.

The legalist would see that as a clear violation of the father's instruction, but Andrea's behavior did not violate the principle of caring for her dad's car. Context allows a child to do the right thing even if situations change. Failing to teach principle deprives the child of moral discretion.

The Bible represents ultimate authority and moral sufficiency. In its pages are the moral virtues that reflect God's righteousness and wisdom. There are no moral variations in its precepts. The values that govern conduct and define good and evil are the same for all people and for all time. As a parent, you need to realize that it is not enough to teach your teen how to act morally; you must also teach your child how to think morally. To accomplish that goal, you yourself must think in accordance with biblical values. That thinking is crucial to the process that you have begun–the process of raising a morally responsible child.

Questions for Review

1. Parents often tell their children what is wrong and what not to do, rather than what is right and what they should do. How does this type of training lead to moral compromise?

2. With whom should moral training begin? Please explain.

3. What is the moral mandate of Scripture?

4. Explain the difference between knowing how to do right and knowing why something is the right thing to do.

5. What is context and why is it important in parenting?

Why Teens Don't Talk or Listen

I.   Introduction and Review

II. Three Methods of Communicating Intent

    A. Parents train by _____, both verbally and by example.

       1. General _____

       2. Moral _____

    B. Parents request by asking a _____.

    C. Parents require compliance when giving _____.

       Instructions are either

       1. _____: We direct our teens to do something.

       2. _____: We restrict our teens from doing something.

III. Principles for giving Instruction

    A. Principle One
       Parents should _____ what they mean and mean what they
       _____.

Undermining your efforts by being a:

1. _____ parent

2. _____ parent

  B. Principle Two

Parents should consider the _____ of their instructions.

  C. Principle Three

Parents should allow for the _____ process.

IV. Principles of the Appeal Process

  A. The Basis for the Appeal Process

  B. The Need for the Appeal Process

It prevents _____ from being unintentionally abusive.

  C. Activating the Appeal Process

The teen must activate the appeal process by providing _____ information that the parents did not have prior to giving their instruction.

  D. Guidelines for Making an Appeal

1. An appeal must be made to the _____ currently giving instructions.

2. Parents should only entertain an appeal when the teen comes with a _____ spirit and not a demanding one.

3. The appeal process is a _____, not a way to avoid objectionable tasks or to get out of personal responsibility.

4. If the appeal process is to work effectively, parents must be _____ and _____.

E. How to Teach the Appeal Process

1. Work through this lesson and your workbook.

2. Set up some scenarios.

3. Use the natural consequence of their choice to reinforce your training.

8

Why Teens Don't Talk or Listen

We have all heard something similar. "When she was little, I couldn't even go to the bathroom without her talking to me through the door. Now, she hardly says a word to me."

The frustration and hurt in this mom's voice as she shared made it clear that communication is an important part of relationships. Speaking and listening are God-given abilities that enable us to verbally express feelings, utter sound with meaning, and write words with intent.

God understands our need for communication. He himself is a communicating and conversational God. The Bible abounds with examples of this. The Lord spoke to Adam and Eve in the garden, the child Samuel in the temple, Moses from a burning bush, and many others throughout Scripture with hundreds of uses of the phrase: "the Lord said." Not only does God speak, but He listens. He listens to the cries of His people and hears their prayers. He's not only the creator of communication, but He's the supreme example of its use.

In contrast, we can all improve our skills. We can listen more attentively and speak more graciously to one another, perhaps most of all with our teens. In this chapter, we will address common mistakes parents make in speaking and listening to their kids. This will set the stage for addressing the how-tos of improving two-way communication, which we will address in the following chapter.

PUTTING COMMUNICATION INTO PERSPECTIVE

It is important to note that simply improving communication is not a relational fix-all. Communication has become a catchword in discussions about troubled marriages and struggling parents. While a lack of communication usually is a symptom of an unhealthy relationship, it is not necessarily true that the poor communication caused it.

Being a skilled communicator doesn't guarantee family harmony or healthy relationships. Communication skills are not a substitute for common or shared values. What holds families together is the moral unity found within the soul of the family. Moral intimacy among family members has no substitute, no backup, and no replacement.

Until we cultivate principle-centered relationships within our families, our efforts to improve communication will have little permanent value. Good speaking and listening skills are an important part of a healthy relationship, but they are not a substitute for it.

Knowing how to communicate with your spouse and kids is important, but even more important is first learning how biblically to love and live with your family. Unconditional love not only should be the basis of our communication, but it is also the ultimate way we develop the rapport that characterizes healthy families.

Without Scripture's moral compass, our conversations can easily get turned around and lost in a wilderness called self. Communion of hearts and minds takes place between persons of like character. People who are morally like-minded get along better than people who are not.

WHY TEENS DON'T TALK

It doesn't take a professional counselor to figure out that good communication enhances relationships, while its poor counterpart signals relationship problems. Like the mother at the beginning of this chapter, we intuitively know something is wrong when our teens shut us out, but we don't always know what that something is. The best place to find our answer is from teens, so we surveyed a number of them. Like us, you may find their answers to be extremely enlightening. Below are the five reasons they gave for clamming up.

"My Dad and Mom Don't Talk to Me."

Some parent-teen conversations never go beyond exchanging facts or giving instructions and correction. This is the lowest level of communication and occurs because parents are satisfied merely to receive or give data. This may be due to the busyness of the day, the rush to get dinner on the table, or the desire to head out the door for a meeting or event. But for whatever reason, parents sometimes don't pursue content in their conversations with their teens. Unfortunately, communication will not improve as long as the parent is satisfied to let it remain at this level.

Gathering facts pertaining to your child's day is important. Some small talk is necessary, but if that is the only level on which you communicate, don't be surprised if you get this type of exchange:

"How was your lunch today?"
"Okay."
"How did you do on your quiz today?"
"I dunno."
"Where are you going tonight?"
"Out."
"Out where?"
"I dunno."
"Do you know when you're coming home?"
"Nope."
"Do you have your homework done?"
"Yup."

What is the cause of this sort of interchange? Which came first, the shallow conversation or the shallow relationship? We really need to talk to our kids about matters of the heart, not just the mundane details of day-to-day existence. Healthy communication goes far beyond the fact level of conversation.

"My Folks Don't Listen, Anyway."

Sometimes teens get the impression that it is never the "right time" to talk with their parents or that they'll never get mom and dad's undivided attention during a conversation. Parents don't intend to send unavailable or half-listening messages, but they frequently do. Preoccupation with jobs, chores, other kids, and even church can leave a teen feeling like everything else is more important than he or she. Sharing dad or mom's attention with the newspaper, TV, computer, or grocery list is a put-off and a putdown.

There will be times when you can't talk "right now," but it's important to make time to do so whenever you can. During those times when you do talk, do you listen fully and with focused attention? Listening with your eyes is as much a part of the conversation as listening with your ears. If your eyes are watching your younger child or focusing out the window, you're only half listening. Teens become acutely aware of this. In such cases, not communicating at all produces less frustration for them than talking to a parent who only half listens.

"They Answer Before I Even Finish Talking."

I, Gary, have failed my children this way on a number of occasions. The Bible says, "He who answers a matter before he hears it, it is folly and shame to him" (Proverbs 18:13). There were times when I thought I knew where a conversation was headed and jumped in with both feet, only later to realize the horrible truth: I had violated this proverb.

Like many parents, I had listened only long enough to get what I thought was the gist of what my child had to say and then quickly offered a solution: "Okay, this is what you need to do." One half of my mind was listening; the other half was assessing the situation and deciding the solution.

Adolescents (and children) can quickly tell if you are really listening or are just surface listening, and they will respond accordingly. After all, would you want to keep talking with someone who rarely gave you the chance to speak your thoughts completely before hitting you with an ill-informed response? Probably not. Our teens don't like it either and will tend to avoid conversations of this sort. We need to focus on what our children are trying to say and let them get it all out before offering a response.

"We Never Agree, Anyway. So Why Talk?"

There may not be any cannons being shot, bullets zipping through the air, or covert sabotage taking place, but comments likes this make it pretty obvious the parent-teen relationship is in a state of cold war. In war, continual conflict shuts off healthy communication, and differences of opinion are perceived as threats.

In stress-filled families, conversations can quickly turn into arguments. As a result, both parent and child tend to pull away from each other, silently agreeing that it is preferable not to talk than to openly wage war.

Silence in the family is unnatural. It is a defense mechanism used not only by struggling parents and teens, but also by those in unhealthy marriages. To be silent is to be in control even when emotions are raging just below the surface. A point on our Family Profile Test in the first chapter sums up the conversational low in many homes: "If it were not for sports or the weather, we probably wouldn't have anything safe to talk about to our teen." But even those topics can produce an argument in some families.

"There's Nothing to Talk to Them About."

This condition is often the result of the independent family structure discussed in chapter 8. When family relationships are optional, talk is optional. The independent family structure affects communication in two ways.

First of all, the nature of independence breeds in-home isolation, not camaraderie. As a result, when there are problems or stress, the teens turn outward to their peers, not inward to their family. This is not only because peers are more available; in many cases, they are viewed as more credible.

Also the independent family fails to provide the opportunities that normally bring families together. Meals, bedtime, and family activities are regrouping times that allow for conversation. When you don't provide the environment for talk, talk doesn't happen.

WHY TEENS DON'T LISTEN

They hear the words of a new pop song while we hear only the loud jumble of guitar chords and drum beats. They listen for hours to their friends on the phone if we let them, and they catch the sound of a friend's car when it drives up. But sometimes our teenagers don't seem to hear one word we say.

Talking is only half of the communication story. Many parents and teens talk to each other but don't always manage to communicate. There may be an exchange of words but not necessarily the sharing of information. Without someone hearing, reflecting, and responding to what is said, words mean little. Parents struggle in frustration when they feel their teens "tune them out." Here's why some sons and daughters told us they do it.

"My Folks Don't do What They Say; So Why Should I Listen to Them?"

"You're such a hypocrite!" This accusation usually triggers an immediate response from parents–anger, justification, or pain–often because there is some truth in the statement.

It is not easy to match our lives to our words, but that is our point of integrity or lack of it. Also, parents who don't live by the moral values they set up for the rest of the family come across as untrustworthy. In the sentence above, the key word is moral.

During the early years of childhood, parental authority, although challenged, is not questioned in terms of parental integrity. Parents tell their children not to cross the street, light a fire, let the dog run loose, or climb daddy's ladder. Yet parents do these same activities without their actions being perceived as hypocritical because these activities are not moral in nature. But when it comes to moral instruction and moral behavior, no disparity should exist between what parents teach and what they do. The moral rules the child is taught to live by are the same for the parent. Adulthood does not come with a new set of values. Moral truth does not vary with a person's age.

Teens make moral judgments on the behavior of friends, schoolmates, and teachers using the standards taught them by their parents. It should not surprise us when our teens use those same standards to judge us.

"I've Already Heard it a Dozen Times."

Nothing makes a teen tune out faster than constantly "reminding" him or her about faults or responsibilities. Homework (and chores) are often a case in point. Frequently, no ground rules are established, or if they are they are not enforced. That leaves mom and dad repeatedly saying things like: "Is your homework done? Your math grade is slipping. You need to discipline yourself. This is your responsibility..." Or how about the endless complaining about the half-frozen cat that was left out all night, due to a teen's forgetfulness? The matter is brought up at breakfast, dinner, and again on the way home after youth group. It is revisited as the cat is tossed out the back door to take care of business before the family retires for the night. The lecture about the poor cat drones on and on.

There is more to communicating with your children than lecturing on what they did wrong–again. Certainly, mistakes and sinful acts must be confronted, but if that is the only time you talk to your teen, plan on being tuned out.

By the third "lecture," your son or daughter does know what you're going to say even if you phrase it differently. They stop listening. Overtalk is communication overkill. We need to communicate effectively in order to teach the values governing personal responsibility, but harping or nagging is not an effective training method.

"My Parents Are Sarcastic. They Just Put Me Down."

In an effort to draw attention to their teen's behavior problems, some parents use sarcasm in their daily conversation as a tool of coercion. Listen for the verbal barbs. "Of course you eat healthy enough. Those potato chips are a vegetable." "So, what kind of trouble did you get into at school today?" "When you act that way, I'm surprised you have any friends at all."

It's difficult to get teens, or anyone for that matter, to listen when they are treated disrespectfully. Teens don't forget put-downs. Turnoff words and put-down phrases force one of two reactions from teens. Either they verbally attack the source of irritation with their own sarcasm, or they withdraw in silence. In both cases, the results are the same—the teen stops listening.

Some parents use sarcasm because they think it will help motivate their kids. But teens resist this type of "motivation" and become cynical of anything the parent says. This has a downward-spiraling effect. New efforts the parent puts forth to make amends are seen as just another twisted effort to control, not build relationship. So the teen tunes out in revenge. To tune out is to take control.

"I Know Just as Much as My Mom and Dad Do."

Teens can sense when parents are unsure of their own beliefs or leadership decisions. This doesn't mean a parent can't say, "I'm not sure how to answer you. I need time to think it through." But it does mean that once the decision is made, parents know their reasons why and stick to them.

Too often we get into the habit of making decisions without thinking them through. Then we start waffling, "Well, maybe this time..." When this happens repeatedly, teens tend to acknowledge the parent's instruction but do what they please. They stop listening because they don't believe their parents are sure of what they are saying or that they have the resolve to enforce it. This teen has greater confidence in his own ability to make decisions than in his parents'. He or she becomes "wise in his own eyes" (Proverbs 26:12).

When a parent says, "If you do this, such and such will happen" but it doesn't happen due to lack of parental resolve or failure to follow through with discipline, it causes the teen to further become wise in his own eyes. Before your teen will listen and follow your instructions, he or she needs to know you believe your own words.

"My Parents Don't Expect Me to Listen."

Parents sometimes expect too little out of the relationship with their teen. They think it's normal for teenagers to be in constant conflict with them and that not talking and not listening are inevitable parts of adolescent behavior.

As mentioned earlier in this book, our society expects teens to resist parental leadership and defy any infringement on the teen's autonomy. Instead of promoting the idea that great relationships can be had with our teenage sons and daughters, we are faced with a nightmarish stereotype of parents pitted against teens in a lose-lose contest of wills.

When we adopt any or all of society's expectations, it affects our parenting. We set rules and say things based more on a stereotype than on who our teen actually is. This can't help but cause him or her not to talk or to listen to what we say. And the more powerless we feel to direct our child's life, the greater the tendency is to lead by controlling than lead by our relational influence. As a result, the relational cycle spirals downward to the point where there is no talking and no listening.

However, the reverse can also be true. Parenting to the true nature of our teens can promote talking and listening. When you truly get to know someone and they know you want their best, your efforts on that person's behalf make you safe to talk with and credible to listen to.

This concludes our study of the common mistakes we as parents make in talking with our teens. Now let's look at the how-tos of improving two-way communication.

Questions for Review

1. Why isn't good communication a guarantee of strong family relationships?

2. Look up Proverbs 18:13 and write down the communication principle it states.

3. The independent family structure affects communication in two ways. What are they?

4. Of the five reasons why teens don't listen to their parents, which one do you struggle with the most? Which is not a problem for you?

9

Bridging the Communication Gap

Not long ago, we asked a young woman who'd just celebrated her twentieth birthday why she hadn't rebelled during her teen years. Put on the spot, she said, "I think for me, it came down to trusting what my mom and dad said and knowing they listened to what I said."

Healthy proactive communication is one of the best forms of adolescent encouragement. Good communication can prevent more conflicts than corrections can solve. A teen's vocabulary and self-understanding is more mature than when he or she was a child. They now can more readily express inner, abstract feelings. This makes adolescence an opportunity for meaningful talk. You can learn how to talk so your teens will listen and learn to listen so your teens will talk.

Communication serves as a vehicle to transfer thoughts, emotions, feelings, and ideas, but it doesn't just happen. We must work to perfect the skills that bring legitimacy to our words and a willingness on the part of our teens to listen to us.

GOD'S GUIDELINES

The first priority of open and honest communication with our teens is to create and maintain a climate of trust so they feel secure enough to talk. This involves submitting ourselves to the biblical ethics governing how we speak and listen.

Proverbs 15:1 speaks to the tone of our words: "A soft answer turns away wrath, but harsh words stir up anger." Colossians 4:6 encourages us to employ well-chosen words: "Let your speech always be with grace, seasoned with salt, that you may know how you ought to answer each one." The ethics of Scripture also govern listening. Proverbs 18:17 teaches us not to listen to just one side of the story: "The first one to plead his cause seems right. Until his neighbor comes and examines him." James 1:19 tells us: "Let everyone be quick to hear, slow to speak, and slow to anger." None of us will master all of these principles all of the time. But these communication guidelines are from God and, therefore, must be followed to the best of our abilities.

There's a tendency to feel God's ethics are good ideals but impossible to practice consistently. Remember, God made language a learned skill. And though we get our grammar or word choice wrong from time to time, we don't stop speaking English. It is valuable to our lives. In the same way, God made His ethics so we can learn them. We might blow one from time to time, but that doesn't mean we cease striving. They are too important to our relationships.

GUARD YOUR TONGUE AND TONE

One day, fourteen-year-old Connor came home from school with great news: the teacher had selected him to be first-chair trombone in his seventh grade band class. That evening when his dad came home from work, Connor ran into the kitchen and shouted, "Guess what, Dad! I made first chair!" Overcome with enthusiasm, he let his imagination soar and cried out, "I'm going to be a musician when I get older."

The feelings this announcement evoked in his father ranged from shock to sincere concern regarding his child's future. "Not if you want to make any money, you're not," he said sharply.

Connor's face fell. He hung his head and turned away. As his father watched him retreat from the living room, he realized he had made a grave error. His son had tried to share with him something that was of great importance to him. In his rush to protect his child, Dad had stolen the joy from his son's heart. In that moment, Connor did not need an analytical assessment about his career aspirations. He needed to share his accomplishment. He wanted his dad to enter into his sense of excitement.

Remember these two rules of thumb when responding to your child of any age: learn to measure your response against the excitement on his or her face, and most of all think before you speak. That is what is known as guarding your tongue and your tone.

We wish someone had shared this principle with us when we were young parents. Gary remembers the morning his young daughter Jennifer came running into the house with an enormous pine cone. In her desire to share this discovery, she set the item in question on the kitchen table and exclaimed: "Dad, look at it! "Her entire face was glowing with excitement, and she wanted to share that feeling with him.

In that moment Gary failed her and himself. What Jennifer saw was a beautiful treasure. What Gary saw was a mess. Disturbed, he turned to her and said, "Jennifer, get that thing off the table. It's full of ants and sand and goo."

In that moment he saw those words destroy a special moment in the life of his child. As he watched the joy and excitement drain from her face, he asked himself why? Why that tone? Why those words? Since that time he has learned this vital lesson: When your child comes to you with excitement and joy written on his or her face, make sure you guard your tongue and tone and learn to measure your response against the excitement on their face. If we fail our kids in their moments of discovery, we potentially lose more than the moment—we lose our children's sense of security and trust in knowing they can share life with dad and mom.

DEEPER MOMENTS

The primary times of talking in the Ezzo household were at dinner and bedtime. When our kids were younger, we talked more at dinner than at bedtime. But when they were teens, we talked more at bedtime than at any other time. We made it a point! We had an interesting arrangement. Some nights the girls sat on the edge of our bed, tucking their mother and me in while recounting the day's activities. The next night it was our turn to sit on the edge of their beds and talk.

Our nightly efforts accomplished more than simply providing an extended time to talk. They provided a necessary opportunity to care for our family at a deeper level of communion. All those nights spent sitting on each other's beds, listening to one another, and participating in meaningful conversation ministered to each of us at a deeper level than could have been achieved at most other times. We would interact with each other and try to empathize with what each one said or thought. We connected to each other on a deeper level than was possible with the conversation we might expect to have at other times when we would talk about Dad's day at work or the kids' day at school.

This is a powerful experience. The deep impression of "the family" resid-ing in each member's heart united us in ways that no principle alone can explain. Just as our communion with Jesus Christ is not merely appreciation for the ink and type on the pages of the Bible but is instead a deep and abiding relation-ship such as that of the Father with His Son–"As you Father are in me and I in you" (John 17:21a)–so also is this dynamic, expressed as the talking soul of the family. When talk-time didn't take place for one reason or another, there was discontentment and loneliness among our family members.

Some families do not know what they don't have. They don't realize the value of time–of using their special moments to develop the soul of the family–until they no longer have it.

THE TEN-TALK RULE

One of the great hindrances to communication in relationships is time availability. Sometimes we just can't stop and talk and give our full attention when our chil-dren ask for it. Sometimes they just want to talk, and other times they need to talk–right now. How do we find the right balance between meeting their imme-diate needs and staying focused on the project in front of us, which may equally need our attention?

To find that balance in our family, we used the *ten-talk* rule. It was a privi-lege and a trust to invoke this rule. If our children absolutely and immediately needed our attention, they'd say, "Dad, I need to talk with you, and this is a ten-talk."

Based on a scale of one to ten, ten being most urgent, our children were trusted to grade their own need and tell us. The grading between one and five repre-sented, "I want to talk with you," and between six and ten meant, "I need to talk with you."

The ten-talk privilege was taken seriously. It meant we were going to trust our children to assess the urgency of their need in light of our present activi-ties. Obviously, my time availability when working on a Sunday message is less flexible than when reading a Louis L'Amour western thriller.

Before coming into my office and evoking an eight- or ten-talk rule, my chil-dren gave plenty of thought to what they were asking. Could it wait a few min-utes, hours, or even days? Could Mom answer the question? Our kids knew we trusted them with the privilege of their own assessment. They also knew that we could be trusted to listen attentively and completely when they really needed it. That mutual trust further served to build our healthy communication.

Did they make judgmental errors? Yes, of course. But by teaching them through their mistakes and explaining that their interruption was not as urgent as they thought, they became more discerning.

BE SENSITIVE TO THE SORTING PROCESS

We're all familiar with the saying, "A picture is worth a thousand words." Today, we'd like to suggest to you that the "picture" your teen paints for you while communicating is worth a million words. Why? Because it is through early conversations with Mom and Dad that he or she will begin to sort out life and relationships.

As we have already discovered, your teen is going through a number of transitions—moral, biological, and relational. Often new challenges in life are not easily harmonized with old, well-worn beliefs that have guided the teen's childhood years. Now, life is even more complex. Sorting out the various issues of life is one of the primary tasks to be tackled during adolescence. Often teens talk at a surface level, but confusion lies at another. This is where gentle conversational probing might be handy.

Wendy's Story

Although she didn't see her same age cousins that often, fifteen-year-old Wendy was always glad when their visit was over and they went back to their own house. Her mother picked up on the attitude and began to probe.

Mom: "Honey, every time you know your cousins are coming to visit you're excited. But once they get here, you seem agitated."

Wendy: "Sarah and Kim are so bossy when they come over. We always have to do what they want."

Mom: "Well you know, honey, they are our guests. We want to be hospitable, and they only come for the weekend."

Wendy: "But it bothers me."

Mom   "Yes, it might bother you. But sometimes God brings people into our lives to teach us things. He wants us to learn patience and how to be kind to people who trouble us. All of this is to help us become more like Jesus."

At this point, Wendy's surface message was about her bossy cousins. Mom attempted to work this issue through with her child but sensed that something more was going on in Wendy's heart. She also realized that Wendy herself might not understand her own feelings. The dialogue continued.

Mom: "Honey, is there something more that's bothering you?"

Wendy: "I don't know."

Mom: "But you understand how God can use people, even irritating people to help shape you into the person He wants you to become?"

Wendy: "I know that Mom, but they always want to hang around with Brian and Daddy. I'm just in the way."

Mom: "No you're not in the way. But you have to remember, Sarah and Kim do not have an older brother or a dad living in the house. One of the reasons they like to come here is because they get to share Daddy and Brian with us."

Wendy: "That's what I don't like about them coming. They're trying to get Brian and Daddy to love them instead of me."

Mom: "Oh, honey. No one can replace you. You are very special to your brother and your dad. You will always receive their special love. No one wants to take that away from you. And even if they wanted to, it wouldn't be possible."

In this abbreviated, but true story, it was mom's sensitivity that was able to bring out Wendy's lingering attitude. It is sometimes difficult for a teen who is trying to sort life out, to see beyond his or her own fears. In Wendy's case her fear of displacement kept her from understanding her cousins' tremendous need for the loving male guidance. Mom helped put all of this into perspective for her.

Forcing their way into your teen's rapidly expanding world are new relationships, emotions, attitudes, experiences, and sensations. They come in twisted and tangled and are in need of sorting out.

In the case of Wendy, there were two messages being communicated. When taken at face value, Wendy's initial words seemed to indicate that she was troubled because her cousins were bossy and wanted to spend more time with Brian and his dad. But when mom began to dig below the surface, she found that there was much more to the situation than met the eye.

Listen for unspoken messages like these. Pay attention to all the signals your child is sending through body language, facial expression, tone of voice, and an overall sense of urgency. These nonverbal cues will give you invaluable insights into the message your child is trying to communicate and the issues of life he or she is facing.

EXPRESS VS. VENT

Allowing teens to express their feelings properly is a vital part of good communication. But some people minimize their expression of emotions while others exaggerate them. Emotional displays, either minimized or exaggerated, impact the person receiving them. To mask your feelings is to deny you have them, but to vent them openly without a care for others can lead to painful resentment for all involved.

We send emotional signals at every encounter. The closer we are to someone, the more our true feelings leak out. This truth makes the family a likely place where feelings are vented more than expressed. We have a communications covenant in our family. We will not stop loving each other in moments when feelings of frustration, hostility, and anger escape us.

Healthy families know the difference between expressing feelings and venting them. Sure, there will be days when someone in the family will be in a bad mood, not talkative, and generally unpleasant to live with. Bad days and good days visit all of us because we are human. But how are you generally characterized? How do you respond when you're angry or upset? Are you able to let the rest of the family know what you feel without saying something you'll regret later?

There is a big difference between honestly expressing your feelings and the more explosive method of doing so–venting. Expressing feelings reflects the present state of affairs which may be quite unpleasant, and this is understandable. But venting tends to be exaggerated, explosive, often nonsensical, and belligerent.

The practice of venting as therapy came from the writings of Freud and was carried forward by his disciples. Parents are warned that a child's psychological health depends on his ability to vent his hostilities and anger and to be verbally aggressive when needed, even to the point of verbal abuse. The theory didn't work for Freud, and it doesn't work with children. Furthermore, it doesn't aid healthy communication. We are not implying that a child should not be allowed to share his or her feelings. We are simply stating that these must be expressed in a socially and morally acceptable manner. No self-help is derived from a sinful out-of-control experience. We've all been there before. It's not pleasant, nor is it God-honoring.

We must all manage our exchange of emotions—not prevent, but manage them. Teens should have the freedom to express their feelings and have them acknowledged by their parents. Parents should have the same freedom. In both cases, self-control must be exercised. It helps to set family guidelines beforehand.

EMPATHY: COMMUNICATION'S HEART

One day our daughter came home from high school. From the look on her face to the droop of her shoulders, Gary knew something was wrong. He risked an exploratory statement. "Jen, you look like you're hurting. It's obvious that it hasn't been a good day. I'm sorry about that." She looked at him with a halfhearted smile, "It's nothing, Dad."

Gary decided not to pry into her private world. He remembered on more than one occasion when a person's "Do you want to talk about it?" put him off. Sometimes we need to pick with whom and when we share troubles. His statement let her know that he cared.

Later that afternoon, Gary was weeding his garden when Jenny came outside, pulled up a crate, and sat down. She started sharing about Martha, a new girl she had befriended. It seemed that Martha had also become friends with Jenny's best friend, Sarah. Suddenly, Jenny was no longer included in Martha and Sarah's plans. She had been nudged out and made a third wheel. It hurt.

Jennifer asked, "Why, Dad, after all these years of being best friends, would Sarah just drop me like that? Sarah wears Martha's clothes and her jewelry and goes home with her after school. And she has only known her for a couple of weeks."

"It hurts when that happens," Gary said, "watching your best friend take off with the new kid, especially the kid you introduced her to." Jenny reacted curiously to that statement. It never occurred to her that one of her parents might have lost a best friend in a similar manner. Gary began to reflect on an incident from his own youth.

Afterward Jenny asked, "What do you think I should do?" "Wait, I guess. Give it some time. Don't try to force yourself into the relationship by playing the same game Martha did. That will only rob you of your integrity. Be gracious with Sarah; maybe she will see that real friendships can never be bought with fancy clothes and expensive jewelry. If you and Sarah were really best friends, she'll come back. Real friendships are not forgotten."

For a teen struggling with life, there is no more important resource than a parent with a capacity for empathy. Letting our kids know that we understand what they are feeling because we have been there ourselves serves to tighten the relational ties. It is a concrete way for them to know we truly do understand.

Incidentally, one day a week later, Jennifer came waltzing into Gary's office after school. She wore a smile that lit up the room. She looked at him and with a twinkle in her eye said, "Dad, Sarah wrote me a note today and apologized for being such a jerk. She told me how foolish she had been to think that all of Martha's beautiful clothes and flashy jewelry could ever replace me. She wants us to be best friends like we always have been."

Gary hugged her. Jenny whispered, "Thanks, Dad; you were right. I waited, and she came back." We've lost track of how many times since then that Jenny and Amy have asked either of us, "Did you ever go through something like this?" Empathy breeds confidence in parental counsel. Share yourself with your kids. Share your failures and your successes, your own adolescent hurts and pains. Tell them the stories of your childhood struggles. We all had them. When teens awaken to the fact that "there is nothing new under the sun," and that every generation experiences similar relational testing and trials, they tend to turn to you with confidence.

A note of caution makes me add that sharing our past with our kids doesn't mean we must disclose deep personal information. Past sinful lifestyles are best kept where God put them. "As far as the East is from the West, so far has He removed our transgressions from us" (Psalm 103:12). Revealing without discretion may be unwise and even corrupting. But sharing to communicate empathy can make a big difference in parent-teen communication.

Questions for Review

1. Which biblical ethic of either talking or listening do you feel parents in general most commonly violate? Which ones do you need to work on?

2. What do we steal from our children when we fail to guard our tone and do not measure our response against the excitement on their faces?

3. What is meant by the phrase: "Parents must be sensitive to the sorting process"?

4. Think about this last week with your teen. Write down a time when you did use or could have used empathy to encourage communication.

5. Explain the difference between expressing feelings and venting them. Can you think of some examples of when one of these two forms of expression may have visited your family in the last several days?

SESSION SIX
Discipline Flow Chart (Encouragement)
and Chapters Ten & Eleven

S1

INSTRUCTION

B1

B2

B3

B4 TYPES OF
ENCOURAGEMENT

B5

B6

B7

B8

B9

T1

F1

T2

T3

T4

T5

T6

10

Principles of Instruction

A strong will and emotional nature made Carol's daughter Lisa a handful. At fourteen, most requests and directives seemed to trigger dramatic situations. Initially, Carol reacted to Lisa's behavior, but the resulting conflict made her do some serious thinking. She started to take note of what defused and what exploded each situation. She even began to see a correlation between Lisa's responses and her own methods of instruction.

Over time, Carol learned that Lisa did much better when directives and consequences were discussed before situations arose. To her relief, she also found that by changing her own communication style she was able to reduce the amount of conflict in her relationship with her daughter.

THE STARTING POINT

As we discussed in earlier chapters, developing healthy patterns of communication is basic to healthy parenting. The next principle we want to share is that learning to communicate instructions to our children is also essential to proper parenting. This is because instruction is the starting point of all moral training. In the example above, Carol thought that she was instructing her daughter. But when she took the time to think through their relationship, Carol realized that she was *reacting and arguing* with her child rather than *instructing* her. Learning how to instruct, to coach from the sidelines of your child's life, is essential to a strong parent-teen relationship, but it takes a conscious effort.

The burden of instruction may seem overwhelming to many parents. However, we are not alone in our efforts to train our children morally. Scripture provides us with the guidelines we need. When Solomon penned the book of Proverbs, he referred to instruction (directly and indirectly) over one hundred times. He bonds it with wisdom, right and just living, child training and correction, fool prevention, and a parent's future delight. Clearly and repeatedly, the world's wisest man establishes instruction as the starting point for moral training.

"Fools despise wisdom and they despise instructions," Solomon warns in Proverbs 1:7. But, "Correct your son and he shall give you rest. He will give delight to your soul" (Proverbs 29:17). In this context, the word "correct" means to educate your child. As used here, it doesn't mean to punish but to train. Proverbs 22:6 tells us to "train up a child in the way he should go and when he is old he will not depart from it." Here the word "train" means to initiate learning, to set the patterns of learning, and to cause one to learn. Proverbs 19:18 says, "Chasten your son while there is hope. And do not set your heart on his destruction." The message is clear: If your teen is going to learn, it is your job as a parent to instruct.

MORAL INSTRUCTIONS AND EXAMPLE

To avoid confusion, we must clarify the difference between moral instruction and general rules. Stealing and lying are moral acts. They are equally wrong for parent and teen. In contrast, a ten o'clock bedtime is not a moral obligation but a health consideration. This requirement is for the youth, not necessarily for the parent.

This contrast should heighten your awareness of the importance of being a moral example to your children at all ages. Parental example must support parental instruction. Instruction without example is authoritarian and produces a teen who is bitter and full of resentment. Example without teaching is permissive and produces a teen who is exasperated, insecure, and left to himself morally. Thus, that which is morally right for the teen must also be morally right for the parent.

Parents should train their children by instruction, but not all instruction will be of the classroom variety. We all learn from simple commands which are either directive (telling us what to do) or restrictive (telling us what not to do). It is because we often lack awareness of these instruction differences that problems and conflicts develop.

As a parent, listen to the type of instruction you give. Are you the type who only gives commands? Or worse, do you tend to be the permissive type who never gives any? Do our instructions teach the intellect but not the heart? Do we demand a new task of our teen without showing him or her how to do it?

Most methods of instruction have value and they fulfill a learning purpose. There is a time and a place for each method, but they are usually best accomplished during periods of non-conflict. Moses spoke of this in Deuteronomy 6:6-9 when he said, "These words which I am commanding you today shall be on your heart." Literally, this phrase can be read "as a weight on your heart," implying a sense of urgency. In verses 7 through 9, Moses instructs parents to teach their children diligently and to do it during the course of daily activities. The word teach implies structured instruction. Parents do not merely assist in a child's learning process. When a child is ready to learn, it is mom and dad's responsibility to teach.

The type of teaching spoken of by Moses is not corrective or punitive, but admonishing and encouraging. It is wise teaching directed toward the child while he is standing, sitting, walking, or lying down. We instruct by correcting, admonishing, warning, rebuking, and encouraging. In essence, we are to continuously teach our children all we know about life.

A POINT OF CONFLICT

Learning how to effectively communicate instructions to our children is essential to proper parenting–and to avoiding problems. Many parent-teen conflicts start at the point of instruction. When we consider the vital role of instruction in a teen's life, there are a few facts and elementary principles that should be kept in mind. Following these basic guidelines can prevent stress and increase willful compliance; failure to comply can lead to power struggles and continuous outright rebellion.

Principle One: To Ask or To Tell

When giving instructions, be sure to say exactly what you mean and mean precisely what you say. Parents commonly violate this simple principle. There is no better way to teach a teen not to obey than to give instructions you have no intention of enforcing, or to make requests that are in reality veiled orders.

By telling your teen, "Take out the trash," you are communicating that you have an expectation he or she must meet. If a failure to obey is not met with consequences, your teen quickly learns that obedience is optional. This conclusion is sure to lead to frustration–both for you and your child–and almost certainly conflict.

On the other hand, if you ask your teen, "Would you mind taking out the trash?" you are making a request. In the face of options—taking out the trash or *not taking* out the trash—your teen may choose to leave the garbage in its current position under the kitchen sink. Your expression of disapproval at this point sends mixed messages. Your teen realizes that the options presented were not truly options. Your request was a test… and he or she failed. This situation leads to misunderstanding and mistrust… and once again, conflict.

In the absence of parental resolve, a teen quickly learns the habit of disregarding all requests made. This habit can become so strong and contempt for instruction so confirmed that all threats will go unheeded. Both directive instructions and restrictive instructions require a response of immediate obedience unless otherwise stated in the instructions.

Principle Two: Now or When?

Parents should consider the timing of their instructions. Sometimes timing is as important as the instruction itself. Parental instruction that interrupts or terminates an activity should often be preceded by a warning, "You need to finish up in five minutes. I want you to…"

We all know what it's like to get absorbed into a project, and we know the frustration of having to set aside our efforts without warning. Teens feel this same frustration. A five-minute warning indicates that instruction requiring compliance will soon be coming. Such a benevolent act helps a teen (or any of us, for that matter) emotionally prepare to stop what he or she is doing and be ready to comply. Parental sensitivity of this sort reduces the shock of intrusion and alleviates the tension between the child's desire to continue with an activity and the need to comply with his parents' instruction.

Principle Three: If, Ands, or Buts

Parents should allow for an appeal process. Many times we give instructions to our kids but are not fully aware of the context in which we've given our instructions. Sometimes they create unnecessary exasperation in the child. When we allow an appeal process, our teen has an acceptable, respectful way to handle his or her frustration.

A POINT OF APPEAL

Examples of appealing to authority can be traced in both the Old and New

Testaments. The first chapter of Daniel tells of the young prophet and his three friends who were slaves in King Nebuchadnezzar's court. Their position called for them to eat food forbidden in the Law of Moses. When Daniel made up his mind not to defile himself with the king's food, he appealed to the commander of the officials. Daniel's appeal won him the favor of his captors.

In the New Testament, the apostle Paul appealed to Caesar (Acts 25:11). Later in the book of Philemon, he appealed to the owner of a runaway slave to forgive and receive the offender. Clearly there is a biblical precedent for appealing to authority.

Both authoritarian and permissive parents have difficulty with the appeal process. That is because the authoritarian parent sees authority as absolute, regardless of parental error or misjudgment. The permissive parent, on the other hand, rejects the role of authority altogether and, therefore, has no use for its safeguards.

For those standing between these extremes, the appeal process can help bring authority into focus. To appeal to authority is to acknowledge another's rule in our lives. To be in a position of leadership and to hear an appeal is to accept our human imperfection. Remember, none of us is a perfect parent. We all make errors in judgment. Thankfully, God in his graciousness has provided principles that can help us build strong relationships with our teens in spite of our short-comings.

The Need

Colossians 3:20 speaks to the issue of children and obedience. In the same passage, Paul warns against provoking and discouraging children. The fact is, the very nature of required compliance will often frustrate a teenager, but that does not mean we do away with the standards of acceptable behavior or common courtesies. So how do parents achieve the necessary balance in maintaining order in the home without exasperating their teen? The answer is found in the appeal process.

Discernment dictates that a parent not ask a teen to turn off the television right before a show ends. Nor would a discerning parent ask a teen to put away a computer game if it were near completion. Those are the types of actions that unnecessarily frustrate teens and violate the principle of not provoking our children. Yet, all of us are insensitive at times or don't know the situation, or act from a different point of reference. This is why the appeal process is necessary.

With the appeal process, the teen becomes proactive in providing *new information* that will help the parent make an informed decision about his or her previous instruction. "Mom, I don't want to" is not new information. That is a preference. The appeal process alerts a parent to a different reference point–that of the child.

Caleb was watching an auto racing video that had five minutes left before ending. His mom didn't realize how close it was to the end and told her son to turn off the television and wash up for dinner. In this case, her frame of reference was dinner, which was about to be placed on the table. Caleb's frame of reference was the video, which was near completion. As a result of her request, tension was created. Should Caleb comply by leaving the program, but be frustrated? Or should he risk ignoring his mother in order to satisfy his desire to watch the race's conclusion? Given these circumstances, compliance would leave Caleb in a state of exasperation, violating Colossians 3:21. Yet, if he took a chance and ignored her instruction, his disobedience would violate Colossians 3:20. Either way there is cause for parent-teen conflict. The appeal process bridges the two verses, preventing disobedience and, equally important, preventing exasperation.

When and How?

To activate an appeal, the teen, not the parent, must initiate the process by providing new information. The parent's job is to hear and to act on that information, realizing that "yes," "no," and "maybe" are all possible answers.

Providing a personal opinion is not the same thing as providing new information. Many children offer a commentary, an analysis, or an opinion on parental instruction. However, that is not providing new, factual information which forms the basis of a legitimate appeal.

In the incident above, Caleb should appeal his mom's instruction by saying, "Mom, may I appeal your request? There are only five minutes left on the video. May I finish it first?" With new information, his mom may reconsider the request without compromising leadership.

There is a legitimacy to his appeal and probably no reason why she would not change and say, "Yes, that's fine. When it is done, please wash up for dinner." Now everyone wins. There is no exasperation, no conflict, and no power struggle. Without the appeal process, problems develop easily.

Bob and his family found seats together at a ball game, but Christopher, age twelve, sat several seats away. Bob instructed him to move closer and heard, "No, Dad, I want to sit here!" Christopher's answer challenged authority and created conflict. If Bob repeated himself, he would reinforce Christopher's noncompliance. If he gave in, he would be compromising his authority and parental integrity. The "no" response forced Bob to take corrective measures.

After receiving a verbal admonishment, Christopher explained his frame of reference. "Dad, I sat over there because I couldn't see all the players with that banner hanging so low." Was that a legitimate reason to sit away from the family? Yes. Was it handled the best way? No. An appeal by Christopher could have prevented the entire scene.

Remember, the appeal process is built on the basis of a trusting relationship. The teen trusts the parent to be fair and flexible, and the parent trusts the child to bring new information that legitimizes the appeal process.

The appeal process is not a cute trick to avoid conflict. Rather, it helps develop a lifelong character-building trait. The willingness of an individual to submit to authority is directly related to the fairness exhibited by that authority. In general, life is not fair. Yet parents can be fair without compromising their authority by teaching their children how to approach them with reasonable appeals.

Questions for Review

1. Why do you think Solomon connected instruction with wisdom—a parent's future delight?

2. How can giving your teen a five-minute warning that instructions will follow prevent exasperation?

3. Think about what you want your teen to do tomorrow. Write down how to say what you really mean. Write down your Request and instructions. When would be a good time to give it?

4. Explain how the appeal process can prevent unnecessary frustration with your teen.

5. Think about the last month and write down an incident where the appeal process would have benefitted the situation.

11

Discipline and Encouragement

The hassle wasn't new. Becky expected her teenage daughter's room to be picked up each morning. Yet when she went past the open door to Donna's room one afternoon, yesterday's clothes, towel, and books dotted the floor and bed. Confronting her daughter later, Becky told her, "You know your room needs to be picked up in the morning. Since you didn't do it then, you can do it now, along with the bathroom."

After the work was done, Donna asked to talk. "My room is clean, Mom, but I really feel upset. I kept it picked up all week, and you never said one word. Then the one day I don't get it done, you get on my case. You only seem to notice the bad things I do."

THE BASICS OF DISCIPLINE

At some point Becky undoubtedly asked herself or others, "How should I discipline this messy bedroom problem?" There seems to be a prevailing assumption that if parents can master better methods of punishment, they'll solve their parent-teen conflicts. Surely punishment plays a role in child-training, but in the teen years, it should play a greatly diminished role. Unfortunately, as the story of Becky and Donna illustrates, more effective solutions–such as encouragement or natural and logical consequences–are often missed.

Fundamental to the process of encouragement and punishment is a basic understanding of the term *discipline*. Let's begin by defining the word. Most parents think only of punishment when they think of discipline, but *discipline* is simply a process of training and learning that fosters moral development. It comes from the same root word as "disciple," which means one who is a learner. The purpose of discipline is to teach morally responsible behavior. Since its principle function is to teach morally responsible behavior, it is critical that we as parents understand the basics of biblical discipline. The positive aspects of biblical discipline are synonymous with education and guidance in that they emphasize inner growth, personal responsibility, and self-control. All of these qualities lead to behavior motivated from within your teen's heart (Proverbs 2:19; 4:23).

God's purpose for discipline is precise. It is to bring about the peaceful fruit of righteousness. Hebrews 12:11 states, "Now no chastening seems to be joyful for the present, but painful; nevertheless, afterward it yields the peaceable fruit of righteousness to those who have been trained by it."

Biblical discipline consists of a number of essential principles and actions—some encouraging, some corrective. Various forms of encouragement that complement the biblical process include affirmation, goal incentives, praise, and rewards. The corrective side consists of verbal reproof, natural consequences, isolation, restrictions, loss of privileges, and chastisement. Each activity has purpose, meaning, and a legitimate place in the overall process.

DISCIPLINING MORAL AND NONMORAL BEHAVIOR

Before we get into the specific actions and principles of discipline, it is important to revisit the fact that behavior falls into two categories: moral and nonmoral (or amoral). Learning to swim, tie a shoelace, ride a bike, kick a ball, climb a rope, play the piano, or memorize the multiplication tables are nonmoral activities. They are skills associated with natural gifts, talents, and mental attributes. They are functions of life but not matters of morality.

In contrast, obedience, kindness, honesty, respect, honor, and integrity are the beginning of a long list of moral attributes. Parents need to stay mindful of the difference between moral and morally neutral behavior. Why? Because the encouragement and correction process for developing a personal skill differs from the encouragement and correction process of modifying behavior. They first focuses on a child's natural abilities; the second concentrates on his or her heart.

Learning to ride a bike is a skill, but riding a bike in such a way to avoid hurting someone is behavioral. Learning to swim is a skill, but bullying other children in the water is wayward behavior. It's wrong to treat these equally. One is related to deficiencies in skills, while the other is moral weakness.

Encouraging Nonmoral Behavior

There are three essential elements required in the development of skills: patience, guidance, and motivation. For a child to be willing to invest time and effort in the practice needed to develop a skill, there must be some source of motivation. Parents can help in this area by praise and goal incentives. Often verbal praise goes a long way. It can make a difference to say something as simple as, "Your game has improved a lot, Jeremy, ever since you added ten minutes to your practice time."

These words link encouragement to the cause and effect of your teen's efforts. Tying your encouragement to a specific activity helps the child measure the value of his practice and encourages him or her to continue putting forth effort.

Encouraging Moral Behavior

Moral behavior is associated with the heart. Parents motivate the heart by encouragement and correction. Both activities are important, and neither one is truly effective without the other. In this chapter we will concentrate on encouragement; in chapter 14 we will tackle the how-tos of correction.

THE EXTRA MILE

When you encourage your teen in the context of a biblical relationship, you are offering a powerful motivator for right behavior. Outside that context, however, encouraging words can sound hypocritical. The comments of a father who does not take the time to establish a trusting relationship with his son or daughter become meaningless statements. Hearing an encouraging word is not the same as having an encouraging parent.

Unfortunately, this is an area in which many parents fail, particularly during the teen years. During this time, parents are so preoccupied with getting things under control by continually correcting, they generally forget to encourage. As we all know from personal experience, the absence of encouragement is the same thing as discouragement.

There are a number of ways to encourage teens. Remember the five love languages we talked about in chapter 8? Verbal praise, physical touch, simple gifts, spending time together, acts of service–each expression of love sends the message that we notice what our kids do and we care about them. But encouragement doesn't just happen. No matter which form of it we use, we must take the time to really notice behavior and then single out the positive aspects of it in regard to the individual doing it. Encouragement requires parents to go an extra mile because it forces them to be proactive. Here are some specific ways you can encourage your teen.

With Words

In healthy relationships, verbal affirmation is never redundant. Each of us enjoys receiving a pat on the back or hearing "well done" from someone we respect. We appreciate hearing how our actions pleased or helped another. Teens are no different. Like the rest of us, they are powerfully encouraged when justified praise comes their way.

If we are not verbalizing our encouragement, what message are we sending? "I love you." Verbally encourage your teens in the little things and the big. It's easier to catch their big efforts, but many times it's the daily stuff that makes or breaks relationships. Sometimes a simple "thank you" can go a long way.

Another way to verbally encourage a child is to say, "I need your help," instead of "I want it," or just, "Do this." The humility it takes to ask for help expressing sincere needs elevates the other person.

If you are just getting started on the encouragement side of your relationship, be careful not to qualify your encouragement. Don't say, "Thanks for doing the dishes tonight. Miracles never cease." Or, "You prepared a great meal; too bad it's burnt." Such qualified encouragement is not encouragement at all.

With Touch

The touch of a gentle hand, a tender hug, or a pat on the back all can convey a message of encouragement. Physical encouragement communicates support, whether in victory or defeat. It fills in when words fail or aren't enough.

To hold and be held communicates vulnerability and a closeness that is reserved for trusting members of a family. For those with a struggling relationship with their teens, this may mean starting slowly–simply placing a hand on the son's or daughter's shoulder and saying, "Great game," or "Great job," or "Thank you." At other times, a high-five or a hug may be best. Whatever the case, don't underestimate the powerful influence of physical encouragement on your teenage son or daughter.

Anne Marie was always great at combining words of encouragement and simple but meaningful expressions of physical touch. Sometimes she would just stop the kids, put her hands on their shoulders, and with great sincerity say: "I just want you to know how much I appreciate the way you..." Verbal affirmation combined with physical touch are an unbeatable combination.

There is a tendency to use the encouragement of touch only when we're happy. But if we've had a bad day, believe me, our teens would notice if we put a gentle hand on their shoulder to say so. Consciously or unconsciously, they'd register the added effort and emotional cost the gesture took.

Gift-Giving

Teens relish being appreciated. One way to show this is through gift-giving. Giving a gift in response to a child's act of loving service is a great way to remind the child that you have not forgotten what he or she did.

We have tried to practice spontaneous gift-giving in our home. There were occasions when my wife and I rushed out the door to a meeting, leaving the kitchen in disarray. Coming home to a spotless kitchen without having prompted the girls to clean up created in us an appreciation deserving of more than a simple "thank you." At times like this, the next day Anne Marie would pick up a couple of thank-you cards and write the girls a note of thanks on behalf of the two of us. Sometimes she would slip an inexpensive pair of earrings in with each card.

This cost very little in time or money, yet it communicated our deep appreciation for their kindness and a desire on our part to celebrate our love for them. It also added quality the next time we said "thank you."

Whether you are working on reclaiming a relationship with your teen or just working to improve it, consider saying "I appreciate you" with a simple gift. However, try to avoid some common pitfalls. Don't attach any "strings" or conditions to your gift. Don't just do it because it's in this book. Make it a genuine gift from your heart. Don't give with expectations. If you find yourself saying, "How could you do that after I gave you...," realize you're giving with expectations. And don't use it as a defense during later conflicts.

With Service

Closely associated with gift-giving is saying "thank you" through acts of service. In the incident above, we could also have expressed our thanks by doing something for the kids that we knew they would appreciate—something over and above what we would normally do.

The teen years were hectic in our home, and there were times when the girls' rooms showed it. Although the girls often kept them neat, there were seasons of clutter. Sometimes during these busy times, Anne Marie would clean their rooms. She wanted to say, "I love and appreciate you," in a tangible way. That act of service communicated the value we placed on what our children were giving to our lives. We appreciated it, and they knew it.

Quality Time

A fifth way to show encouragement to our teens is by giving them our time. As parents, we all struggle to balance competing demands. Work quotas, family responsibilities, personal interests, friendships, ministry opportunities, personal interests–all of these and more cry out for our attention.

Your teen may very well be aware of the battle you wage. After all, he or she lives with you. Better than anyone else, your family knows how little time you have to spare. With that in mind, what could be more encouraging than to show up and cheer at your child's drama production, band concert, or soccer game? Or to take your teen to lunch one day, "Just to tell you how proud I am of you for the way you helped your brother study for his test" (made peace with your best friend, prepared dinner on the night that mom was sick).

These are just some of the many ways we can encourage our teens. But don't let the suggestions we've outlined limit you. Remember, any action you do as a parent that instills in your teen the courage to do right is encouragement.

Now let's take a look at the role of correction in the moral training of our teens.

Questions for Review

1. Look back on the discipline of your teen the past week. Was it all corrective? Write down two times when you could have used encouragement to discipline.

2. The literal meaning of the word *encouragement* is "to put courage in." Why do you think your son or daughter would need courage to live morally?

3. Write out one instance you saw in your teen this week that demonstrated amoral behavior. Write an instance of moral behavior.

4. Of the ways we listed to encourage (words, touch, gifts, and service), what is your strongest/easiest way? Your weakest/hardest? What is one thing you can do this week to practice your weakest skill? Your strongest?

5. Write out one way you could encourage each of your teens this week. Remember to make your encouragement individual and sincere.

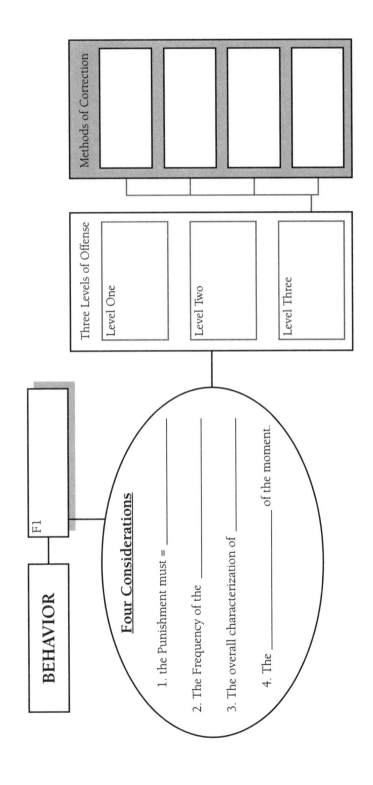

Methods of Correction

Three Levels of Offense

Level One

Level Two

Level Three

F1

BEHAVIOR

<u>**Four Considerations**</u>

1. the Punishment must = _____

2. The Frequency of the _____

3. The overall characterization of _____

4. The _____ of the moment.

12

The Corrective Side of Training

When airliner takes off, the flight engineer determines what direction the pilot needs to steer the plane to get on the desired course. Sometimes the plane gets off that course. When that happens, it's up to the air traffic controllers in the control towers to highlight that and give instructions to get back on course.

So it is with teenagers: Sometimes they get off course. It falls to parents to make sure they can find their way back to the right path.

When a teenager needs correction, it's not something parents go into with the intent to hurt or punish, with no other goal but to cause pain. It's something they do out of love to be sure their teen gets to the right destination. Parents use as much correction as is necessary to realign the teen's course, but no more.

In this chapter we give you principles that will help you on those occasions when your teenager really does need to be corrected. These are tools that have been proven effective in thousands of homes very much like yours. The Nathan parable, especially, is great for those times when your teen may not realize what she's doing is wrong. We'll start with what we call the five laws of correction.

THE FIVE LAWS OF CORRECTION

As we have said, by the time a child is in his teens, you should be leading less through the exercise of your authority. Therefore we will only present the laws in summary form. If you're interested in the fuller treatment, we recommend you pick up one of our earlier books, especially *Along the Virtuous Way*.

Law One

DISTINGUISH BETWEEN MISTAKES AND DEFIANCE

There is a distinction between the fifteen-year-old who accidentally crushes his brother's new CD and the teen who goes on a rampage because he wasn't invited to the beach with his brother's friends. When you're deciding the proper means of correction for a situation, be sure to determine whether the deed was done out of innocence or malice.

In our previous books, we referred to innocent disobedience as *childishness*. It's when the young person does something wrong but wouldn't have if he had known it was wrong or had been able to prevent it. *Defiance,* on the other hand, refers to those acts that are done intentionally to cause injury or loss. Childishness is usually a head problem–a lack of knowledge. Defiance is usually a heart problem–the child does not want to do right.

Parents should make the distinction between mistakes and intentional disobedience and discipline accordingly.

Law Two

ALL CORRECTION MUST PROMOTE LEARNING

Fifteen-year-old Liz knew that only her best friend, Sue, was allowed in the house if her parents weren't home. Liz had once gotten cornered into an uncomfortable situation with too many friends over, making a mess all over the house. So, when Sue stopped over with her boyfriend, looking for a quiet place to be alone with him, Liz let both of them in. It wasn't a group, after all, just two people, and one was Sue. She figured this would be all right.

Mom and Dad, however, had strong opinions to the contrary. Apparently, their original restriction did not promote learning. Liz wasn't able to apply the past lesson to her present situation.

The goal in correction isn't merely to correct a single act of defiance but to prevent it from ever happening again. Many times this can be accomplished just by explaining why the thing was wrong. When you instill into a teen's heart the why of correction, you'll be far less likely to be dealing with that issue in the future. If learning did not take place, correction didn't happen.

Law Three

THE PUNISHMENT SHOULD FIT THE CRIME

As adults, we do not get punished by our parents for our decisions. Our punishment is that we have to live with the consequences of our choices. So should it be with your teen. When your child was young, punishments were appropriate. But when a child becomes a teenager, punishment should play a greatly diminished role. In its place, use natural and logical consequences–modified to fit the situation–to accomplish your correction.

We once heard someone teach that every disobedient act by a child should be punished the same way: by beating the child. But disobedience comes in all sizes and frequencies, so there can be no one punishment or correction that is appropriate for them all. (And children should never be beaten.)

Factors that parents should weigh when considering appropriate correction include:

- the age of the teen (Is this a child who has just entered the teen years or a seasoned veteran of seventeen?)
- the frequency of the offense (Is this the second time or the seventy-second?)
- the context of the offense (Was your child the instigator or a follower?)
- the overall characterization of the child's behavior (Is this behavior unusual or common?)
- the need for balance in discipline (Too harsh brings exasperation; too little breeds contempt)

Law Four

AN OFFENSE AGAINST A PERSON OR PROPERTY REQUIRES AN APOLOGY

Relationships work best when there is no unresolved conflict between them. If your teenager has committed an offense against someone or someone's property (but no monetary damage was done), he owes an apology.

There is a difference between giving an apology and asking for forgiveness. Either or both may be appropriate in a situation, but they are not the same. An apology is a simple, "I'm sorry." This is called for when the teenager has accidentally offended the person or abused the property or if he did so not knowing he wasn't supposed to. In this case a sincere apology is usually sufficient.

But if there was intent to harm or offend, "I'm sorry" won't cut it. Now the teenager needs to seek forgiveness. This means humbling himself before the other person, confessing what he's done, and requesting the person's forgiveness. This requires a contrite, penitent attitude–which, by the way, is a wonderful thing in anyone.

The offended party may not grant forgiveness. They may be too hurt or angry. But that's not your teen's concern. If he presents himself in humility and expresses a willingness to make it right, that's enough. America is full of bitter, unforgiving people. That's their choice. But if your teen has made a legitimate request for forgiveness, he has done what he could and should have to think about it no more.

Why is this forgiveness thing so powerful? Because when a teen merely says, "I'm sorry," she's in control of that moment. She controls the depth and sincerity of her sorrow. But when she seeks forgiveness, the one she's humbling herself before is in control. She's asking something of that person that she cannot get without his or her consent—forgiveness. It is this humbling effect that so wonderfully curbs a teen's (and a parent's) appetite for going back and doing the same wrong thing again.

Law Five

IF FINANCIAL LIABILITY OCCURS, THE TEEN SHOULD MAKE RESTITUTION
In the real world, "If you broke it, you bought it." It shouldn't be any different for your teen. Mom and Dad can't come bail Junior out every time he makes a costly mess. If they do, they'll be doing it for the rest of his life. This is part of instilling into your teen responsibility for his own actions.

Parents can use restitution to teach, too. Make the level of restitution fit the crime. If the teen caused one hundred dollars damage because she accidentally knocked someone's dishes onto the floor, she should work until she could repay the one hundred dollars—or, better yet, until she could replace the dishes. If, on the other hand, she broke the dishes in a vicious tantrum, the restitution ratio should be two-to-one, three-to-one, four-to-one, or even higher. Restitution is a good teacher.

Always remember that correction is not about getting even with our teens but about teaching. The aim is to make the right path clear to your teen and, when necessary, put him back on it.

A BARREL OF MONKEYS
Sixteen-year-old Gina just can't seem to grasp the concept of rinsing off her plate and placing it in the dishwasher. Apparently she believes the burden of carrying her plate from the table to the sink is more than enough for her to bear.

Mom, on the other hand, believes Gina can do a bit more. Yet each evening, Mom watches speechlessly as Gina casually places the plate in the sink and retreats toward her room. Gina is usually halfway up the stairs before Mom's voice reaches her. "The dishwasher, Gina. That's where your dirty dishes belong." Gina stomps back down the stairs and almost breaks the plate as she shoves it into the dishwasher rack.

It's an unpleasant ritual they act out every day. Mom yearns to turn this around. But how? The answer lies not with Gina but with Mom. So long as she's always reminding Gina–and never disciplining her–the lesson will not stick. She's teaching her daughter that there really is no consequence for neglecting this chore, so why should Gina ever do it?

Parents have to transfer the responsibility for correct behavior onto their children. When a child is one, his parents do virtually everything for him. But every month and year that passes should see his parents teaching him how to do more and more himself. One of the main goals of parenting is to raise up a self-governing, conscientious young person who has internalized the responsibility for right attitudes and actions.

Excuse Me, Is This Your Monkey?

If this doesn't seem to be happening with your teen, first look to yourself. Many times, well-meaning parents can contribute to this problem by continuing to do for their children. Do you constantly remind your teen to do things you know she already knows she's supposed to do? Do you hear yourself giving the same prompting for the thirtieth time this week? If so, that's where you need to start. You need to break yourself of this habit and start enforcing penalties for your teen not heeding something she knows to do.

Until parents learn how to transfer ownership responsibility for behaviors to their children, those children have no reason to be accountable for their actions. No child will ever become self-governing so long as Mom and Dad are always prompting. With your constant reminders, you teach your teen that you aren't serious. If the command were something you really needed her to respond to, her failure to do so would create all kinds of consequences. If no consequences ever come, then no compliance will ever come either.

In Gina's case, she knew that sometimes her mom would call her back to the sink and sometimes she wouldn't. Sometimes her mom would do the chore herself. She knew she could wear her mother down. If Mom got too tired to call Gina back downstairs, so much the better. There might be a lingering sense of guilt about manipulating her mother that way, but if she could get away with it, with only the occasional lecture as punishment for disobedience, it was well worth doing.

Constantly reminding your teen to do what is expected only means you have no expectation. When your teenager understands what he's supposed to do and that he's supposed to do it, that should be it. You shouldn't have to remind him about it. If it's a brand-new behavior and he's just not accustomed to thinking about it, then one reminder the first time might be appropriate. But anything beyond that and you risk falling into the habit of always reminding him. Unless your teen has some kind of learning disorder that prevents him from remembering, you should back off.

A parent who constantly reminds a teen to do something he's supposed to do on his own has not transferred responsibility: He's taken it back on himself. Notice that this is not the teen's problem but the parent's. If you want to bear the burden of remembering, he's usually pleased to let you do so. One less thing.

Responsibilities are like monkeys. They like to hop from one person's back to another's. Parents start out with the child's entire barrel of monkeys. As the child grows, his parents begin handing him his monkeys as he's able to take them on. By the time the child is grown, he should be carrying all his monkeys.

A parent who assigns a task, then retains the burden of remembering to do it, has allowed that monkey to jump back onto her. Send them back! Your goal is to get rid of the monkeys not collect them.

Your primary ally in this crusade is a simple little phrase: "Do you have the freedom?"

Monkey Repellent

Sixteen-year-old Jake asks to borrow the car one fine spring day. The guys are starting up a game of hoops over at the gym, he tells Mom. So, Mom thinks quick. No, she doesn't need the car, but aren't there a few things Jake needs to handle before taking off?

"What about the lawn?" she asks. "Didn't Dad say he needed your help with that this morning since company's coming this afternoon? And what about the tools you left out in the garage last night? You told Dad you'd clean them up first thing. Did you do that? Oh, and remember, when you use the car, you need to put a few dollars in the jar on the counter to help pay for gas. Do you have that right now?"

Do you hear the sound of monkeys jumping? Mom's checklist of reminders has yanked those primates straight back onto her shoulders. There's a better way for her to handle this. We call it monkey repellent.

Think of privileges as freedoms. A teen who has earned the privilege of not needing a curfew has the *freedom* to stay out late. Teens gain privileges and freedoms by rightfully carrying out chores and responsibilities. A teen who has not completed his responsibilities is not entitled to enjoy the associated level of freedom. Freedom and self-governance are connected.

Here's how Jake's mom should have answered: "Jake, I know Dad spoke with you last night about some responsibilities. Do you have the freedom to play basketball right now?"

Uh, oh. Now Jake's the one squirming. He knows his responsibilities very well, and now Mom's expecting him to be accountable for them. He may not like it, but he understands that his freedoms are contingent on his obligations. That's the way real life is, isn't it? If you don't get up and go to work every day, you don't get paid. Jake may not realize it right now, but his mom is helping him learn how to succeed in the real world.

The question, "Do you have the freedom to do that?" repels monkeys because it puts the burden of ownership back on the child. It forces him to think. *Well, do I?* Contrast that with Mom's checklist of reminders. Which one do you think will provoke a teen to greater initiative and follow-through?

An additional benefit to a teen learning how to internalize his own sense of responsibility is that he is less susceptible to peer pressure. He has learned to think about freedoms and responsibilities for himself and therefore is not dependent on others to do his thinking for him.

Monkey Business

The typical teen really does want to look you in the eye and honestly say, "Yes, Mom, I do have the freedom to shoot hoops. I took care of the chores and already put a few bills in the jar."

If a teen tells his parents that he has the freedom to do something and in reality he doesn't, consequences are necessary. Let's say Jake's jobs were not completed, but he told his mom they were just so he could get out the door. Upon his return, there would be another discussion.

Of course he would need to get busy doing the chores. But that's not a consequence since he'd been assigned those duties in the first place. There would need to be some further penalty. Perhaps he loses the freedom of playing basketball with the guys for a month. Perhaps he loses car privileges or his open-ended curfew for a certain length of time.

Freedoms and responsibilities are connected. As you learn to pass your teen's monkeys onto him, and as your teen learns to be in charge of his own attention to those assignments, his freedoms should go up and your parent/teen relationship should soar.

SUBSTITUTION VS. SUPPRESSION

Your daughter brings home a CD with objectionable lyrics. You want to march right in there and confiscate the disc and maybe the CD player itself while you're at it. But that may not be the best way to put an end to the behavior that's bothering you.

Your son's asking for an extremely violent computer game for his birthday. It's supposed to have the most awesome graphics and gameplay on the planet, or so he says. He's played it at his buddy's house, so he knows he likes it. You go to the store and watch a demo, and you're sickened by the realistic gore you see splattered everywhere. You're so mad that you're ready to go home and say, "You want some violence? I'll give you some violence." But that might not be the most effective approach.

With teenagers (and adults, for that matter) sometimes we can't just squelch the bad behavior we want eliminated. Simply pulling the plug on an activity or forbidding a relationship may backfire: It is likely to cause the other person to rise up and fight. Then it becomes a battle of wills. You'll be tempted to exert your authority—"Because I said so!"—causing your teen to be sorely tempted to defy you.

There's a better way. We call it using substitution over suppression. If you want to stop your teen's relationship with one group of kids, for instance, you'd better be making friends with families whose children you'd prefer your teen to be with. If you're going to ban one kind of music, do some research so you can recommend some "cool" alternatives. If you want your daughter to stop seeing that boy, maybe it's time for Daddy to come back into the picture since that's probably who she's seeking a substitute for anyway. If your teen is jealous all the time, don't just try to squelch his jealousy, teach contentment and generosity.

You can't just take away something someone cares deeply for and leave a vacuum. There has to be a substitute, something new for the person to put in its place, or he will go back to the old ways. He doesn't know any other way.

It is better to guide your teens away from behaviors and relationships of which you do not approve with substitutes than it is to try to squash those behaviors and relationships by parental decree. The beauty of the substitution method is that not only do you get your teen to stop doing the bad thing, but you have the opportunity to introduce him to something you value and esteem.

THE NATHAN PARABLE

There is an old story about King David, the second king of ancient Israel. Instead of going out with his army to campaign, he stayed at the palace–and got into trouble. As he was strolling around on the roof of his house, he saw a beautiful woman taking a bath. This was Bathsheba, the wife of one of David's loyal soldiers. David sent for her and she came. Thus began a series of events that led to adultery, deceit, and ultimately murder.

At the height of David's folly, the prophet Nathan came to him with a story. He told a tale of an injustice that had been done in David's kingdom. A very rich man, owner of great flocks, had had a visitor arrive at his home. Rather than slaughter one of his own sheep for the guest, the rich man went to his poor neighbor who had only one sheep, a little ewe who was so close to him that he slept with it, and killed that sheep for the meal.

David was furious. "Any man who would do such a thing deserves to die! He must repay four lambs to the poor man for the one he stole and for having no pity."

Then Nathan spun on him and said, "You are the man!"

He showed the king how he had defrauded and murdered Bathsheba's husband for his wife when David's own harem was overflowing. David was pierced to the heart over what he had done. Though he was never again the king he had been, at least he was rescued from complete destruction, and the throne did not pass from his family.

Nathan used a parable to get David to see something to which he'd turned a blind eye. You may find parables a powerful tool to use with your teenager. The appeal of a made-up story like this is that you can show the crucial problem in high relief, holding it up to the light for all to see, but in a nonthreatening way. It's just a story, after all. It's even better if you can get the teen to contribute to the story, saying how wrong that person in the story is. Then, when you get to the end, she has her own words to deal with.

Gary and Anne Marie Ezzo once counseled a couple who had implied that someone was guilty of a certain offense simply based on circumstantial evidence and the fact that they didn't know the accused *hadn't* committed it. Because this couple had made similar insinuations in the past (ones that later had proven to be false), the Ezzos felt they needed to do something to help them see what they were doing.

Instead of confronting the issue head-on, when the Ezzos were with them next they set up a parable. As the unsuspecting couple listened, they began their story:

"This week our car was hit by another car."

"Oh, dear," this couple said. "Was everyone all right?"

"Yes, everyone's fine. It happened at night, while it was parked."

"That's a relief."

"Of course whoever did it drove off without leaving a note or anything. But we think we know who did it."

"How? Did someone see something?"

"No, but we can tell it was hit by a white car because there's white paint in the dent in our blue car. When we took it to the insurance company, they asked us, 'Do you know anyone who owns a white car?' And we said we did because you two own a white car, don't you?"

They didn't answer right away. "What are you saying? Are you suggesting that we hit your car and drove off?"

The Ezzos shrugged.

"Well, that's preposterous," the couple said. "I can't believe we're hearing this. We would never do something like that and then drive off."

"I know you say that, but you do have a white car, don't you?"

"Yes, but that doesn't—"

"And we don't know that you *didn't* hit our car."

"But we didn't!"

"So you say. But we went ahead and told the police that we were pretty sure it was you."

The Ezzos did eventually tell them it was only a parable, but it certainly got the point across. They were able to see with absolute clarity how they had damaged reputations and friendships by their reckless accusations.

If you suspect your teen is doing something wrong or if you want to present the dangers of something your teen is doing, consider using a Nathan parable. You can tell it as a real story, as perhaps something that happened at work today, or you can make it clear that it's just a made-up story to illustrate something.

When you come to the *You are the man* point, be sure to retain your gentleness without sacrificing your clarity. Chances are, when you take the curtain away and reveal what you've been saying, you and your teen will have some talking to do. Maybe you got something wrong, or maybe it's not the way you were thinking at all. But as long as you're talking, it's a good thing.

SUMMARY

By the time a child becomes a teenager, she's developed most of what her personality and identity are going to be. There will still be a need for correction, just as a pilot makes minute course corrections as he's flying. And there may be times when unexpected turbulence disrupts the smooth flight. But as long as you keep in mind the five laws of correction, keep the monkeys where they belong, substitute rather than suppress, and use parables, you should stay well on course and arrive at your desired destination.

Questions For Review

1. What is the primary difference between childishness and foolish defiance?

2. Fill in the blank: "If learning did not take place, _____ didn't happen." What does this mean?

3. What is the difference between an apology and asking forgiveness? What's so powerful about seeking and granting forgiveness?

4. What is restitution, and why is it such a good teacher?

5. What is the monkey repellent phrase, and why does it work?

6. In your own words explain the concept of substitution versus suppression.

Answering the Questions

I.   Introduction and Review

II. Dating Issues

Dating is a Western phenomenon that allows our children access to a serious relationship reserved for courtship.

III. Hair, Clothing, Music and Peers

IV. Series Summary

13

Answering The Questions

We provided this series of questions and answers as a supplemental resource to the first twelve chapters. We trust you will find it of value to your unique situation. Of course, we are not in your home. We can only give general answers. Sometimes they will not apply in your situation. Our hope is that we can at least get you in the neighborhood of something that will help. The principles we use should fit your situation even if the specifics don't.

Also, all parents are at different places in their parenting. Some people on the rapport/conflict scale we introduced in Chapter One have it pretty easy. Their biggest problem is they can't get their teen to turn off the lights in his bedroom. Other people are dealing with more grave matters: drugs, sexual activity, crime. Again, we believe the principles we present here can be scaled up or down to fit most situations.

The questions are divided according to general categories listed first. We trust you will find them, helpful and encouraging.

POPULARITY, PEER PRESSURE, AND SELF-IMAGE
- My teenager is starting to hang around with the wrong crowd. What can I do?
- My teenager would do anything to be accepted by the group. Should I be worried?
- My teenager is very popular in school, but I'm getting reports that he (or she) is unkind to those not in the right clique. Is it my place to say anything?

- My teenager is not the most attractive or popular person in school. She tries to be accepted by the popular kids, but they only ridicule her. What can I do?
- My daughter doesn't think I notice, but I'm beginning to suspect she's got an eating disorder. How can I be sure? What can I do to help?

SCHOOL

- Public schools are getting so violent. Should I put my teenager in a private school?
- My teenager is tormented so badly by other kids at school that it's a struggle just to get him (or her) to go. What can I do?

COLLEGE AND CAREER

- My teenager is so unmotivated in school now, why should I believe things will be different in college? Why should I spend money I don't have to send an unmotivated teen to college?
- My teenager wants to go into professional sports (or into a career in the arts), but I don't think he's got the talent to make it. How do I get him to think realistically without squashing his dreams?
- What guidelines can you give me about jobs—full-time, part-time, after-school, and summer jobs?

DRUGS AND ALCOHOL

- By the time my child was eight, he'd been confronted with drugs, guns, sex, pornography, theft, alcohol, and homosexuality. Do you think this is why he struggles so much as a teenager?
- My teenager is a good kid. I don't have to worry about drugs or alcohol, do I?
- I'm thinking that my teenager should try a little of everything, just to see what it's all about. That way it's easier to know if something should be accepted or rejected. Is this a good plan?

REBELLION

- I didn't discover your books until too late. My teenager is in complete rebellion. I'm so afraid and angry and hurt. What can I do?

- My teenager won't even talk to me. How can I work on the great communication suggestions you make in this book?
- My teenager is showing signs that he doesn't respect me anymore. What can I do to regain my authority?
- My teenager doesn't openly defy me but rather pushes the limit a bit. If I say be home by ten, she's home at ten-fifteen. Do I have grounds to be upset?
- My teenager came home with a certain part of his (or her) body pierced. What can I do?

DISCIPLINE AND CONTROL

- My teenager gets angry when I ask him (or her) to do chores around the house. What can I do to feel like I'm still in charge in this home? (Am I still in charge?)
- When he's with me, my teenager is well behaved. It's when he's not with me that worries me. How can I be sure he's acting properly when I'm not around?
- When I try to discipline my teen, he just gets into his car and drives off.

VIOLENCE AND CRIME

- Although I can't prove it, I suspect my teenager has broken the law, perhaps more than once. I don't want to turn my own child in to the police. What should I do?
- Ever since my husband and I got divorced, our teenager has been acting out violently. How can I help if reconciliation is not an option?
- My teenager has mentioned suicide a few times. Should I take it seriously?
- My twelve-year-old son has drugged me numerous times and tried to kill me. I'm not kidding. I can't live like this anymore. Help! He also leaves the pool gate open purposely, hoping to encourage our three-year-old daughter to go for a swim at the bottom of the pool. He has admitted his motives. I've worked through *Preteen Wise* and a host of other books and courses. What can I do short of having him arrested and taken from our home?

THE MEDIA, INTERNET AND COMPUTERS

- I'm so fed up with my teenager's media choices that I'm just about ready to cancel cable, throw away the TV and the radio, break some CDs, and sell our computer. Before I go on my rampage, is there a better way to react?

- My teenager plays video games from the moment he gets home from school until I force him to go to bed at night. I'm thinking things are a little out of control. Am I crazy, or could he be addicted to that thing?
- Can the various forms of media be the source of our relational tension with our teen?

SECTION 1: POPULARITY, PEER PRESSURE, AND SELF-IMAGE

1. My teenager is starting to hang around with the wrong crowd. What can I do?

The reason we never think our kids are hanging around with a bad crowd when they're in third or fourth grade is that those kids didn't look so bad back then. They seemed pretty normal, though perhaps not particularly well behaved. Now, when those same kids are sixteen or seventeen, we wonder how we could have missed it. Your child may be hanging around with the very same kids, only now you see the glaring moral disparity that was almost invisible before.

We get nervous when we look at these kids and see the signs of where some of them may be headed in terms of the trouble they could potentially get into. We know we don't want our kids to get there. But from the child's perspective, nothing's changed. These are still the same kids they've always hung around with.

Any approach you take to attempt to lead your teen away from these peers must rely on the power of your relationship with your teen. You need to sit down and have an honest talk about the types of behavior that are right for your family. If your family has established a common moral stance, you can appeal to that. Point out some of the more dangerous aspects of particular lifestyles. Hopefully, your teen will agree with you that there is a disparity between what those friends are like and what your family stands for and will see the need to make a break.

But don't do it in time of crisis. When your teen says, "Mom, can I go over to Matt's house today because we're going to spend the weekend together?" that's not the time to say, "No, I don't like Matt." Your timing is probably as important in these conversations as the words you use. When talking about any important issue with your teen, make sure you operate in periods of nonconflict.

Keep the concept of substitution over suppression in mind (see Chapter 12). If you're going to attempt to suppress a relationship, make sure you're ready to substitute something in its place. If you're going to tell your teen that these are not the best kids for her to hang around with, you'd better be establishing relationships with families that have great kids. Provide a natural alternative. You simply can't cut off relationships with your kids without providing them with a substitution.

Sit down with your teen and have a talk. Ask her what qualities draw her to these friends. Then ask how she feels these qualities and these friends are going to help her reach her goals in life. As kids get into the teen years, you want them to come to their own conclusions. You provide guidance, but you don't make the decisions for them. It's so much better for your teen to say, "Yeah, maybe this guy really isn't the best one for me to hang around with," than for you to dictate that to her. When your teen realizes for herself that someone is a bad influence, she'll be more willing to break off that relationship. But if you dictate with your authority, you're just asking for strife.

2. My teenager would do anything to be accepted by the group. Should I be worried?

Sometimes it's a good thing to want to be accepted by the group. Peer pressure isn't always bad. If it's a positive group, with values you agree with, then it may be applying positive peer pressure on your child. He may clean up some behaviors just because of his new friends.

There are personality, temperament, and love language variables that may make your teenager predisposed to want to be accepted or close to a group. However, if you're pretty sure that isn't the case with your teen, you should try to determine what it is that is motivating him to want so badly to be accepted by this group. We all need to feel accepted and appreciated. But if a teen is willing to do nearly anything to be accepted, it may be cause for alarm. Help your teenager evaluate exactly why this is so important in his life that he's willing to compromise who he is to be accepted by them.

You may find that this is really a need for more time with Dad or an indication that you've got an independent family as opposed to an interdependent one. Or there may be some deficiency in the child's self-perception. If he feels his own identity will be enhanced by just being friends with these people, then you as his parent need to deal with the root issue (the lack he feels in his own self) rather than the symptoms.

3. My teenager is very popular in school, but I'm getting reports that he (or she) is kind to those not in the right clique. Is it my place to say anything?

It's always your place as a mom and dad to be a moral compass. This behavior, if true, calls for correction. In chapter 6 we talked about how correction simply means "putting back on track." This situation does not necessarily call for discipline. It may be more appropriate to provide moral correction. Point out how his actions may be hurting others. Consider using a Nathan parable.

Isn't it wonderful that your teenager is well accepted? If you have a child like this, you have the opportunity to instill graciousness and empathy. Teach your popular teen to reach out in kindness and gentleness to those who don't have everything he has. A teen who is friendly to those who are less popular is attractive in a way that transcends nice looks, clothes, and teeth.

4. My teenager is not the most attractive or popular person in school. She tries to be accepted by the popular kids, but they only ridicule her. What can I do?

Usually when your teen desires acceptance by a certain group, it's saying more about your teen than about the group. The key question is why your teen feels she has to be accepted by this particular group. Sit down and talk with her. Ask her what it is this group offers that she desires. What would she gain if she were accepted by this group, and what would it mean about her if she weren't? Listen for clues about what she feels she's lacking that she thinks this group would provide. That's where you should focus your efforts to help your daughter.

The hard truth is that life is not fair. Not everyone will like your child. Young people can be terribly cruel to one another. If this group is rejecting your daughter, it may also be because of insecurities of their own, because confident people welcome new friends easily.

Take this opportunity to gently teach your child. Rejection hurts. Right now, she's feeling like the outcast. But that won't always be the case. Help her to understand that she will often be in a position of accepting or rejecting others. Now that she knows how awful rejection feels, she can determine to reach out to others in the future. Have her seek friends from outside the "in group." She may find that there are more neat kids outside the in group than inside.

5. My daughter doesn't think I notice, but I'm beginning to suspect she's got an eating disorder. How can I be sure? What can I do to help?

Eating disorders are serious business. There are specialists in this area who can give you information that will allow you to evaluate and attempt to understand the problem. There is also good information available on the Internet. The first step is to get educated. If, after you've learned a bit, your suspicions seem to be confirmed, consider taking her to a specialist.

Eating disorders usually have at their root a sense that the young person has failed to be accepted by people who are close to her, especially her father. If your daughter is showing signs of an eating disorder, Dad needs to get more involved, if at all possible. It is amazing what one bicycle ride, one walk in the park, or one trip to the mall with Dad can do for a daughter who is developing symptoms of any of these disorders.

Dad, pick up a copy of *Along the Virtuous Way,* and read the chapter called "The Father's Mandate." That chapter illustrates a child's need for a healthy relationship with Dad and gives practical ideas for how to build one with your children. In a case like this, parents need to concentrate on purposefully expressing their unconditional acceptance of their teen. If they realize they *haven't* been extending unconditional acceptance, then that's where they need to start working.

SECTION 2: SCHOOL

1. Public schools are getting so violent. Should I put my teenager in a private school?

We often hear the sentiment that public schools are terrible, private schools are better (but expensive), and homeschooling is the "safest" option (though not without problems of its own). But this isn't true across the board. There are some wonderful public schools, some scary private schools, and some unhealthy homeschool situations.

The number one consideration for moms and dads is their teen's moral and physical health and safety. Until we come to a place in our society where we have a common level of human decency and protection for all, we are going to be faced with hostility in some public schools. If you or your teen feel he is not safe where he is, consider making a change.

Because of the tragedies in several public schools, many parents are considering private schools for their kids. But these can be expensive, and they're not right for every teen. If your teen goes to a private school, she may have to give up a lot of great activities and sports that are offered at the public school. On the other hand, the student-to-teacher ratios are usually better at private schools, and they tend to give more attention to character.

Homeschooling might be an option to consider. This movement, once popular primarily among Evangelical Christians, has now become quite fashionable in the mainstream culture. However, as with private schools, homeschooling isn't for everyone. It's a lot of work for parents, not all of whom feel they can adequately teach their children, especially at the high school level. And let's face it, not all parents want to have their teenagers around them that much.

Talk to your own teenager about the issue. Some teens will say, "Yes, please get me out of this school." They recognize the struggle that's going on, and they actually would not mind being homeschooled. That might sound like a foreign concept, but we've met some teens who were willing to move out of a public school just because of the violence they were seeing around them.

The good news is this doesn't have to be a once-for-all decision. It's sometimes a good idea to try all three—homeschool until age seven, for instance, private school through ninth grade, then public school until graduation, or some other arrangement. Keep tinkering with your options until you find what's right for your teen and your family at this time. Evaluate it every semester.

2. My teenager is tormented so badly by other kids at school that it's a struggle just to get him (or her) to go. What can I do?

Kids who have been raised morally are often attractive targets for those who have not been raised that way. Living according to a high moral standard will always make a teen stand out. It can become very uncomfortable when the culture of the school militates against what a teen stands for.

What can you do about this? Well, you're certainly not going to not teach your teen to be responsible or respectful or moral simply to avoid ridicule. You must give your teen confidence and tools for dealing with this kind of harassment. You may also want to evaluate whether your teen is in the right school situation for this time in her life.

This scenario demonstrates the need both for a strong family identity and for a moral community. These will give him the ability to resist peer pressure and will give him some like-minded friends to stand with in the struggle.

SECTION 3: COLLEGE AND CAREER

1. My teenager is so unmotivated in school now, why should I believe things will be different in college? Why should I spend money I don't have to send an unmotivated teen to college?

A lack of motivation in school may be a behavior problem or it may not. Some temperaments have a greater desire to please and achieve than others. We don't want you to feel that if you have an unmotivated teen that you're a terrible parent. One of us (Gary Ezzo) gave his parents a very hard time because he was simply unmotivated when it came to school. If he wanted to do something, he had all the motivation in the world. But if someone else wanted him to do something, he wasn't interested.

Gary says: "My family had two apple trees. Every year there was one Saturday when my brother and I had to rake up the apples that had made it through the winter but had fallen in springtime and begun to rot on the ground. My brother had no problem doing this chore. He would just take that rake and get the job done. But I had a tree, too. I just didn't want to rake those apples. There were other things in life I really wanted to do besides rake apples. So I would just wait it out.

"I have to say I don't think my parents handled this situation correctly, because I knew that if I didn't rake those apples, someone would eventually come and do it for me. I was more motivated to ride it out than to do the work even though it wouldn't have taken me fifteen minutes to do it."

Believe it or not, there still are children like that. If you've got one and you're considering whether or not you should send him to college, you should make sure your expectations are realistic. Whether your teen is unmotivated because of temperament or behavioral deficiencies, the results may be the same. Some parents choose to allow their teenagers to wait on college until they've gotten some direction for their lives and proven their willingness to help pay their way through school.

The key for parents of an unmotivated teen is not to try to break him of this but to find out what it is that does motivate him. Draw from the unique gift-edness and personality of the teen to find the secret for getting him moving. If you can tap into that, the motivation problems may disappear.

Or you can always try to scare your teenager straight by giving him a dose of what life without a college education might be like. You can teach tomorrow's consequences today. That's what Gary's parents did. Here is his story.

Gary's Father and Mother worked in a shoe factory. When each of their sons turned sixteen, they had them spend their summer vacation working in a very inhospitable portion of the same factory. It was not a pleasant experience. The summers were hot, there was no air conditioning, and in those days, no OSHA. One of Gary's jobs was to work the oil-wheel room where full pieces of cow hide soaked in hot oil, laid in large wooden wheels. Gary's job that summer was to jump into the wheel and remove the one hundred pieces of oil-soaked leather. He did that ten times a day, all summer long.

Every afternoon it was the same routine. At 4:30 p.m. he would drag himself out to his parents' car and wait for them. Fifteen minutes later his parents joined him. His Dad would get into the car, look at the pathetic heap in the back seat and ask: "How was work today, son?" Gary responded, "Fine Dad." And then his father would remind him of his future: "Son, you will go to college and make a better life for yourself or you will work in a factory like this the rest of your life." That summer Gary experienced tomorrow's potential consequences everyday in an oil room.

If your teen is unmotivated for college, consider putting her into a voca-tion. Give her a job before you send money off to school. It may be that she never goes to college. There is a misconception that if your kids don't go to college, they won't be able to make it in life. But we know many people who never went to college and are making more money than many Ph.D.'s.

2. My teenager wants to go into professional sports (or into a career in the arts), but I don't think he's got the talent to make it. How do I get him to think realistically without squashing his dreams?

This is a tough one. You have to handle your child's dreams with care. But you also want to equip him to succeed in life. Sometimes the problem will solve itself. After a season of interest in music or hockey or whatever, your teen may decide he's not that interested after all. But if your teen is nearing the end of high school and is talking about pursuing the art or sport through college and beyond, it might be time for parents to gently intervene.

First, be sure you evaluate your child accurately. Get the opinion of others qualified to judge. If there really is unusual talent there, you may actually want to step up your support of the activity. If there is only a moderate amount of talent, you may want to begin thinking about other paths he might take. If there is raw talent but no determination to excel, your teen doesn't have a chance of making it. He would be better off coming to grips with that now rather than later.

Consider giving your teen the opportunity to investigate an activity. Let him play for a season or do repertory theater for a summer. If, after a fair time of investigation, your teen hasn't demonstrated the requisite talent level or commitment, you need to help him face the reality that this may not be for him, at least not as a career.

Even with talent and determination, it's very often not enough to make it in careers in sports and the arts. Free agent tryouts in pro sports and open auditions in the performing arts are overflowing with talented and determined people. Gifted, trained, and experienced players and performers are a dime a dozen. There will usually be twenty people more qualified than your child for every available spot.

We think our schools, especially our high schools, do children a disservice by giving unreserved encouragement in the areas of sports and the arts. Teenagers are trying to figure out what they want to do in life. If they excel in basketball or dance, teachers and parents will encourage them to pursue it in college. They communicate the message that the young person "has what it takes" to make it in this field as a career, when in actuality what this teen may have is the talent to stand out at the high school level. High school standout talent is not the same as successful career talent.

So these teens go to college where, not surprisingly, there are degree plans in sports and fine arts (often taught by former high school standouts who didn't have the ability to make a career out of doing it and so have turned to teaching). The young adult graduates from college having played on the team or with a degree in vocal performance or theater…and finds he can't get a job. After disappointing tryouts in Green Bay or off Broadway, he begins to realize the hard truth.

Perhaps he thinks back to all those teachers and professors who encouraged him along the way and wonders why they didn't tell him this would happen instead of always painting lovely but unlikely pictures. Here he sits with no marketable skills and a degree no one values. How is he going to support himself?

Parents want to encourage their children, and so they should. We want them to be confident and realize they have something special to offer. But we should also want to help them survive in this harsh, sometimes cruel, world.

Here is the key for handling this difficult situation. In order to encourage your child to follow her dream and yet still be sure she'll be able to support herself if the dream never becomes reality, *develop a contingency plan with your teen.*

Say something along these lines: "Son, you really are gifted in this activity. Your father and I want to help you learn your craft and take advantage of every opportunity to turn this into your career if that's what you want. But we also want you to be able to take care of yourself while you're waiting for your big break. So, alongside the classes you take to hone your skills in this area, we want you to take classes in computer programming or accounting or business management, something that will help you get a well-paying job to support you while you work to make your dreams come true."

With a plan like this, you can show your support of your child's aspirations and also be sure she is taken care of over the long haul.

3. What guidelines can you give me about jobs—full-time, part-time, after-school, and summer jobs?

There are two primary scenarios when it comes to teens and jobs: They either want one or they don't. Here are some guidelines for both situations.

If your teen wants a job, be it an after-school job or a summer job, the first question to ask is why she wants it. Is it for money or status or approval? What is the money going to go for? Is she hoping to earn some extra cash to fund her CD-buying habit or is she saving up to move away from you? Do you think the money will go for pizza or for drugs? Is there a rebellion issue at play? If so, that needs to be what you address first.

Jobs can be great teachers for the real world. You can use a job to help your teen learn how to manage money, how to be a responsible employee, and how to value a dollar. In real life, if you don't work, you don't have money to spend. An after-school or summer job can help drive this home. It can be an excellent way to transfer some more monkeys onto your teen's back. He can begin to assume responsibility for his own clothing purchases, car fuel and upkeep, and whatever extras he desires.

The second question you need to ask is whether a job would be the best use of your teen's time. If it's a summer job, would summer school serve her better? If working on a skill or sport might give her a better chance of receiving a scholarship, maybe a job wouldn't be the best option right now.

Third, will this job interfere with schoolwork, family time, or other responsibilities? If the cost is higher than the family is willing to pay, it might be better to wait on the job. You might consider just trying it for a while to see if the benefits outweigh the costs. If it turns out that they don't, you can reevaluate.

The second scenario is when the teen doesn't want a job, but Mom and Dad want him to get one. Teens work hard during the school year, often taking on sports and arts and other extracurricular activities that can add up to sixty-plus hours of activity a week. When summertime comes, they can want to just crash for two months before starting it all over again.

We understand. However, in the real world, they're not going to get nice two-month vacations every year. If they're lucky, they'll get a week. After they've been there twenty years, maybe they'll work up to three weeks in a year. Allowing teens to have such a big vacation does not do them any favors in terms of equipping them for life.

That doesn't mean your teen doesn't need a vacation. Try to incorporate some rejuvenation time into the summer. Maybe allow a week or two break between school and the job. If she can find a job with flexible hours or in which she'll be doing something she enjoys, so much the better. It's a balance. Help out by discussing the options and laying out parameters.

One mother told her teenage son he had to get a summer job working at least twenty hours a week. When he moaned about it, she gave him another option. "Okay, you don't have to get a job; you can work for me. I'll give you at least twenty hours of work every week. But I only pay twenty-five cents an hour." Needless to say, he was motivated to go find a part-time job.

Jobs can be wonderful tools for parents to teach hard lessons about what makes the world go 'round.

SECTION 4: DRUGS AND ALCOHOL

1. By the time my child was eight, he'd been confronted with drugs, guns, sex, pornography, theft, alcohol, and homosexuality. Do you think this is why he struggles so much as a teenager?

The things children are assaulted by today are unbelievable. They're introduced to hard-core vices at ever earlier ages. James Dean's bad boy character in *Rebel without a Cause* defied authority by racing jalopies and smoking. That same kid today has been a drug dealer for five years, has had multiple sexual encounters with multiple partners, has made crack addicts of every preteen he knows, and has shot at someone in anger.

Kids just aren't ready to deal with these things. They don't even know long division, but they have to know how to say no to free crack samples. They're having to grow up way too fast, and parents must give them the skills they need to cope or they risk losing them.

Your best ally in your battle to protect your child is a community of like-minded families. A moral community, coupled with a strong family identity at home, is the magic bullet, the secret pill that can both decrease the amount of temptation assaulting your child and help regulate him when he's not with you.

We don't mean you should isolate your family or your child from society, but that you should provide a safe community that is shielded from certain destructive forces. If you surround yourself with families who hold to the same ideals you do, you provide an environment of protection that can insulate your child from the terrible things he might otherwise have to deal with.

2. My teenager is a good kid. I don't have to worry about drugs or alcohol, do I?

This sounds like a naive question, but believe it or not, there are some parents who can say with confidence and accuracy, "My kids would never get involved in drugs or alcohol, certainly not on a long-term basis." These parents aren't "lucky," they've worked hard to be able to say this.

You may have done a wonderful job in raising your son or daughter, but every parent should still be wary. It doesn't take much to become physiologically addicted. Without the support of a moral community and in the presence of overwhelming peer pressure, even good kids can make wrong choices.

We live in a society that is consumed with the quick fix, the immediate high. Drug use has been glorified by music, television, and movies. It's got its own subculture, dress, and language. Someone looking for an identity different from the one he has could find it in this drug culture, especially if it offends Mom and Dad.

When your child goes to college or moves out of your home, you will not be there to monitor his behavior. So, even if you know your teen hasn't experimented with drugs or alcohol, before he leaves your home, you need to sit down and have an earnest discussion about it. "Honey, what's going to happen when you go off to college and some of the guys in the dorm say, 'Hey, why don't you just try this? It's really not so bad'?"

If a teenager hasn't had some dialogue beforehand, no matter how moral he is, he's *human*. "What would it hurt just to try it once?" So many times it's the good kid who ends up getting hooked because he didn't have any defenses in place.

Why not have this talk with your teen today?

3. I'm thinking that my teenager should try a little of everything, just to see what it's all about. That way it's easier to know if something should be accepted or rejected. Is this a good plan?

The idea that teenagers should try everything is fallacious reasoning. Should they really try drugs to know that drugs are bad? How much experimentation with pornography do you want your son to do before he realizes it could be addictive? How much experimentation do you want your daughter to do with sexual activity before she realizes this is not right for her or for her body, or before she gets pregnant?

We like the story of the father whose children pleaded with him for permission to see a certain movie. It had their favorite actors, there was only a little sex in it, and the violence wasn't as bad as a lot of other movies. Besides, everyone else was seeing it. The father said no and remained firm. Then he went into the kitchen.

An hour or so later he offered his children some hot brownies. He'd used all their favorite ingredients, he explained: chocolate and eggs and flour and sugar. The children were reaching for brownies when he explained that in making them he'd mixed in only a tiny bit of dog poop. There wasn't as much in them as there could be, and they probably wouldn't taste it at all. Besides everybody else was eating brownies just like these.

Teenagers don't have to taste something to know it's not good for them. Parents are supposed to advise their children. They are there to teach them that certain things can hurt them. If you saw a mother letting her toddler play unattended by the freeway, you'd say that mother was irresponsible. Would it change your opinion if she explained she was doing it so he could find out for himself that playing by the freeway is dangerous?

Use your position as parent to save your teens from mistakes you could have kept them from.

SECTION FIVE 5: REBELLION

1. I didn't discover your books until too late. My teenager is in complete rebellion. I'm so afraid and angry and hurt. What can I do?

There is a false notion in our society that, at age eighteen, your kids will cease to be your children and you can no longer influence them. Chances are, you're going to live the next twenty, thirty, even forty years on this earth, so you'll have decades with your adult children. You may have not had the best years with your children in the past, but you've got the rest of your life to make it right.

Begin by evaluating your own parenting to be sure you're not contributing to the problem. Then start working on rebuilding trust and influence. You haven't found this book too late. As long as you and your children both live, it's never too late to rebuild your relationship. Go back to chapter 1, and start rereading this book.

2. My teenager won't even talk to me. How can I work on the great communication suggestions you make in this book?

If you can't stand to look at each other because you know you're going to break out into a fight, then why not just slip a note under her door? It doesn't have to be a long note, and it certainly shouldn't be accusatory. Write something as simple as, "I really do love you. I'm just struggling, and I know you're struggling, too." And don't be surprised when a note comes flying by you when you've got your hands in the dishwater.

Sometimes we communicate better when we're not face-to-face. We can become so antagonistic to each other as parents and teens. Our physical presence reminds us of a hurtful word or a hurtful action, and before we know it, we're screaming. These walls can be broken down with just a simple note.

We would also recommend that you go back and reread the chapter on love languages. If you learn to express your love in ways your teen can understand and you persevere in doing so, eventually you will win through. Sometimes just placing your hand on your teenager's shoulder and saying, "I really appreciate what you've done," can break down a wall.

3. My teenager is showing signs that he doesn't respect me anymore. What can I do to regain my authority?

Usually the lack of respect for a parent has been there all along; it's just that the way a teenager demonstrates disrespect is more visible, especially now that the teenager is the same size or bigger than the parent. Sometimes a teen feels a greater sense of security in himself, like maybe he doesn't need to give respect to the parent anymore. In all probability, respect has been missing for a long time.

Your goal shouldn't be to regain dominance over your teenager but to achieve influence. It's natural to want to control something that's out of control, especially when that something is your child. But when you have teenagers, using force won't get you where you want to go. You have no good options besides working to lead by your relational influence.

One area you'll want to work on is freedom. Not the unrestrained, do-whatever-you-want type of freedom, but the kind of freedom in which your teen is emancipated to communicate and to be his own person without the fear that an authority figure is going to force him to become something other than what he is.

It is also possible that you have misinterpreted your teen. What you are hopefully headed toward with your teenager is a peer relationship. But neither you nor your teen knows exactly how to act as equals. What you've interpreted as a lack of respect might be your teenager's first attempt at friendly familiarity. She might be teasing you.

It's usually quite clear when a teenager means to show disrespect. So, if you're not sure, and if your child usually doesn't speak this way, you might at least ask yourself whether you two are just reaching a point in your relationship where you feel you can have a little bit of fun.

Don't try to regain control. Work instead on regaining your teen's respect and trust.

4. My teenager doesn't openly defy me but rather pushes the limit a bit. If I say be home by ten, she's home at ten-fifteen. Do I have grounds to be upset?

Assuming this happens regularly and without good reason, this is what we call micro-rebellion. When your child was four and you told her to stay on the carpet, did she stand with her foot on the carpet but her toes poking over onto the tile? When she was ten and you asked her to put her dirty clothes in the hamper, did she toss them near the hamper?

As we say in *On Becoming Preteen Wise*, for this young person micro-rebellion is full-scale rebellion. Parents may tend to dismiss this kind of rule bending as minor, but it is not minor to the child. Her toe may only be partly over the line, but her heart is completely over. Rebellion of any size, uncorrected, leads to contempt for authority. A micro-rebellious child who has not been corrected in the early or middle years is going to reveal the true depths of her rebellion as a teenager.

It's also possible for parents to unintentionally raise up a child who does not respect their instructions. When your son was five, how many times did you ask him to pick up his toys? If he delayed picking them up or did not pick them up all the time, did you finally do it for him? When he was nine, now many times did you have to ask him to put his bike in the garage before he finally did it? Did you nag? Did you threaten punishment but never follow through? If so, is it any wonder that your teenager doesn't think he needs to do what you ask?

Correct this problem by following our suggestions for how to regain influence with your teenager. Eventually you will want to confront your teen about his micro-rebellion. But be sure not to do it in the heat of the moment. When he strolls in at ten-fifteen is not the time. But you might want to talk about it tomorrow morning over cereal and coffee.

While the time for authoritative parenting is over with this child, it's never too late to mean what you say. If you set a curfew for your teenager, there has to be a consequence for breaking it. Otherwise, it's not a rule; it's a suggestion. It's time to grow a backbone, Mom or Dad. If your teen breaks the curfew without a good reason, enforce the consequence. A parent who does not follow through on promises will be despised.

There is something better than a curfew: trust. When the relationship between parents and teens is very good, certain rules become superfluous. The Ezzos set no curfew for their daughters. Because the girls had proven themselves trustworthy in the small things, their parents were willing to trust them in this.

But it wasn't a blind trust. It was a courtesy trust. It had parameters on it. The girls would tell their parents what their plans were and when they expected to be home. If those plans changed, they called home. But even in those conversations there was a mutual respect. It wasn't, "Hey, Mom and Dad, this is what we're going to do, so deal with it." It was a dialogue.

5. My teenager came home with a certain part of his (or her) body pierced. What can I do?

Every generation comes out with new fads to shock old folks. It was shocking in the fifties to watch the Fabulous Four come over from England with long hair. It created a rage: Suddenly, long hair was in, and the good, Republican, short haircut was out. It also created an outrage: People were talking about it, preaching about it, writing editorials on it. Long hair was thought to herald the decline of the American ethical system. Now long hair is mostly out and short hair is in again.

In the seventies, young girls started to wear bracelets around their ankles. Originally, that was the symbol for a prostitute, so parents didn't want their daughters wearing anklets. In time, it became just a style option and no longer carried the connotation of prostitution. It became culturally acceptable. The same is true for men wearing earrings or ponytails. Once it was done for rebellion; then it passed into the mainstream and became just a fashion choice.

These days the rage is tattooing and body piercing: nose, lip, tongue, eyebrow, belly button, etc. There is a shock value here. Many times a young person will adopt this style to express rebellion or nonconformity. Eventually, tattoos and body piercing will pass into the mainstream. Young people will get things painted or pierced simply because they truly believe it looks good. Some would argue that this transition has already taken place. Indeed, we know several delightful teenagers who have had their belly buttons pierced.

We think health concerns justify some limitations on body piercing. For instance, tongue piercing is out: You can't eat, and there's a danger of infection. If your teenager is considering body art or piercing, another thing you may want to discuss is the very real possibility that this style may go out of fashion. What may be considered attractive in ten years is a body that doesn't have pierce holes all over it. "Honey, just think about this: You might meet someone in a few years whom you'd dearly love to marry but who is totally turned off by the fact that you once had your nose pierced."

The question you have to ask when your teenager comes home with some body part pierced is why she did it. Was it done to offend authority or flout the establishment? Or did she do it just because her friend Julie did it, and it's the latest style? If her motive is to keep up with teen fads, that's one thing. But if she's done it out of insolence, the matter is more serious.

The teenager who comes home with something pierced in order to shock you is saying, "Hello, where have you been?" The pierced tongue, lip, nose, or eyebrow is your teen's way of telling you there is a disparity between who he is and who you are. When you see it, your tendency will be to give a knee-jerk reaction. "What in the world have you done!" That may, in fact, be the teen's goal: to at least get you to pay attention to him. You do need to deal with it, but we would advise you wait until you're cooled down.

When your teen does something like this to show he or she is rejecting you and your values, your inclination may be to strike back: "How can I hurt you for hurting me?" But that won't get you anywhere. Your teen is crying out to you that something is wrong, and he wants you to fix it. Otherwise why would you be the target of his shocking fashion statement? Just as suicide is so often a cry for help, so something like this is often a cry for attention.

Your question has to be, "How do I win him back?" That's going to be hard. The process will probably take months. You've got to regain the love, confidence, and trust of your teen. This gets back to the whole premise of this book, which is that you're going to fix most teen problems through the strength of your parent/teen relationship.

SECTION 6: DISCIPLINE AND CONTROL

1. My teenager gets angry when I ask him (or her) to do chores around the house. What can I do to feel like I'm still in charge in this home? (Am I still in charge?)

First, evaluate what you are doing. Sometimes moms and dads, out of love and pure hearts, can find themselves doing everything for their children. Do you still clean up the dishes for them at dinnertime? Are you still pushing his chair in when he gets up from the table? Are you still making his bed and picking up his socks? Teens won't typically take ownership responsibility of behaviors if someone is always there reinforcing noncompliance. You may have to break yourself of certain habits before you'll be able to instill new, healthy habits into your children.

In chapter 12 we talked about responsibilities being monkeys. Your children's monkeys love to jump back onto your shoulders. Your job is to instill in your child the responsibility of doing the chore himself. If you don't use the monkey repellent we discuss, you'll quickly be weighed down by countless chimps. We would encourage you to refer to that chapter.

A teen's refusal to do simple chores may be a symptom of a more serious problem than habit. You may just want to go back to the beginning and reread this entire book.

2. When he's with me, my teenager is well behaved. It's when he's not with me that worries me. How can I be sure he's acting properly when I'm not around?

Do you have just cause to believe your teenager is behaving poorly when apart from you? Are neighbors and school officials and other parents coming to you with similar negative reports about your teen? If you're getting a series of reports that are alarming to you, then do not let your teen's good behavior in your presence prevent you from exploring what is going on in his or her life.

Any of us is capable of making wrong choices from time to time. What you should be searching for is whether or not your teenager is characterized by this kind of misbehavior. Are you dealing with someone who acts out once every three years or once every three hours?

We should always think the best about our children. If your teenager feels you're waiting around the corner for him to fall so you can accuse him, you're not going to do anyone any favors. We should be expecting them to do the right thing. Your teen should feel you're counting on his good behavior, not waiting for misbehavior.

If it becomes clear that your teenager is behaving improperly when not in your presence, then you've got a high hill to climb. This goes back to what we said about not being able to leave your child at home alone. Until you can be certain of his behavior and until the bad reports stop coming in, you may not be able to leave him alone for extended periods.

But as you work through the principles in this book and your relationship with your teen sweetens, you may find this problem taking care of itself.

3. When I try to discipline my teen, he just gets into his car and drives off.

It could paralyze you to think that if you said something your teen didn't like, he might get into his car and flee. He could drive around the block, or he could take off across the country and you'd never know. On the other hand, if you allow this behavior to scare you into silence, your teen's temper tantrum has been successful.

There's not much you can do in the moment. Your words will be few. If he drives off, he drives off. Just pray that he is safe until you have the opportunity to talk again.

In the meantime, go back to the beginning of this book and start applying some of the basic relational principles we've talked about. Start enhancing your marriage. Sit on the couch with your spouse and talk. Learn your teen's temperament. Learn yours. When he comes home, have a heart-to-heart talk, and continue these regularly as you move forward.

If you are making the payments on this car and if you are paying the insurance, it's appropriate for you to make decisions on how it's used and who uses it. Consider taking the keys away for a while.

While you're both sitting around the house wondering what to do, go for a walk together. Have a meaningful conversation over a meal or dessert. What America's teens are missing are moms and dads who take the time to talk with them. Parents work in hopes of giving their kids a great financial future. But you don't need to do that. Your kids will make a future for themselves if you give yourself over to them right now.

SECTION 7: VIOLENCE AND CRIME

1. Although I can't prove it, I suspect my teenager has broken the law, perhaps more than once. I don't want to turn my own child in to the police. What should I do?

This situation might be best handled not by direct accusation but through a parable investigation. Use the Nathan parable as your model to set up a story that captures the essence of what you suspect your teen of doing.

Let's say you suspect your son has been shoplifting. Perhaps you could design a hypothetical story about what happened at work today. "Son, I work with Mr. So-and-So. Just before five, I saw him take some pencils and pads of paper from the supply closet. I know he didn't take them to use them at work because I saw him get into his car with them and drive away. I think he's taking them home to his kids. I'm wondering about the rightness or wrongness of this. Son, tell me, what should I say to this man?"

Then, when he says it's definitely stealing, you can start bringing it around to the *you are the man* side. "So, it's wrong for someone to take things that don't belong to him and bring them home for personal use?" Eventually, your teen may realize what you're saying. That's when you should address the issue of what should be done: "Okay, so what should this person do now to make it right?"

2. Ever since my husband and I got divorced, our teenager has been acting out violently. How can I help if reconciliation is not an option?

Divorce will affect children differently according to a number of variables, such as their age, personality, temperament, birth order, which parent is leaving, and the longevity of the problem.

Consider the temperament of your teen. If he is very quiet and internalizes everything, that's how he will handle the divorce. He might become extremely sensitive, going into a tailspin at the slightest provocation. On the other hand, a teenager who is vocal and demonstrative about his emotions is going to be that way about the divorce. He may begin responding violently. Sometimes this will explode suddenly and then be over; other times it will be a continued pattern of destructiveness–to himself, others, or both.

Another factor is the longevity of the problem. If it's been going on a long time, there will be a root of bitterness there, an endless wellspring of negative outpourings. A child who has been aware of his parents' problems building for years, all the time wondering if his world is going to hold together and finally seeing that it isn't, might erupt into violence.

If your teen is acting out violently, we suggest the following six ideas. First, in quiet moments, help her work through the grieving stages that a child will go through with any great loss. Divorce is a loss: a loss of familiarity, a loss of a parent, a loss of an imagined future. There will be anger, denial, bargaining, and the rest. Divorced parents have to deal with grief, too, so why not work through it together?

Second, provide stability. Your teenager's universe has just come unglued. That's enough change for anyone to handle. Don't change everything else in the process. If it's at all possible, stay in the same house, and let your child keep his own friends and stay in his own school. Keep familiarity around wherever you can. Let as many things as possible remain fixed.

Third, listen to your teen. If you never had talk times before, now's the time to start having them. If you've had them all along, have twice as many now. If your teen feels she's not being heard or if you are closing her out, too, she may resort to more destructive means to get your attention. Your teenager needs you to have time for her.

Fourth, be around stable families, families in which there is both a husband and a wife at home. Encourage your teen to visit friends who come from stable homes. It's not that single-parent families are to be avoided, but simply that problems sometimes propagate problems. Sometimes things rub off onto your teen from the families he's around. Try to be sure what rubs off will be healthy things from stable families.

Fifth, provide an atmosphere of forgiveness. If every time you speak with your teen you're talking about your lousy ex, you'll be feeding him anger and frustration. He probably still has a child's devotion to that parent even though he knows some of what's happened. Your accusations mount up against his loyalty and create a riptide in his heart. No wonder he's acting out. You need to work through your own anger (leaving your children out of it) and arrive at forgiveness. Then begin encouraging your teen to forgive, too. She will need to forgive the other parent, you, and most likely herself.

Sixth, find someone to lean on. Get good counsel from someone you trust. Find someone for your teen to lean on, too. If there is a stable same-gender family member or friend who can be there for the child, make arrangements for that to happen on a regular basis. You're not trying to replace the parent who has left, but just to give your teen even a few crumbs of Daddy or Mommy time.

Even if you do all this, some kids just won't be able to handle it. Some will act out violently, others will get into drugs, commit crimes, and get pregnant (or impregnate). If that happens, tell your teen that if he's going to go overboard, that's his choice. But that you will be there for him when he comes back around and needs you.

As we have maintained throughout our books, the best situation for a child is to have a father and a mother who love each other and are committed to the family. Any other state of affairs is less than ideal and places serious obstacles in a child's path to healthy adulthood. But if divorce does come, use these suggestions to lessen the pain.

3. My teenager has mentioned suicide a few times. Should I take it seriously?

You should definitely take it seriously anytime a young person makes a threat to himself or others. Especially since suicide has been so glorified by the media. People think this will be their way to have their day in the sun. The problem is that the one who commits suicide never knows whether or not he had his day.

These are the types of things that you may want to mention to your teen's teacher, your clergy, or a school counselor to get advice and verification. You also need to get educated. Counselors have a whole checklist of behaviors to watch for. This will help you identify the potential warning signs of a teenager who is suicidal. Start being observant. Is your child becoming more isolated, cutting off ties, being removed from friends, becoming more moody, locking himself into his room?

Do not take a chance. The best thing that could happen is for you to find out that your teen was just talking about suicide to get your attention. If so, evaluate how you might be able to devote more talk time to the relationship. It would be a tragedy if you ignored legitimate warning signs. When someone mentions suicide, she is usually crying out, "Would you look at me? Would you help me?" It's not always that she really wants to end her life, but that she's just asking for someone to come to her aid. If you were not to respond to these cries, that could be the straw that breaks the camel's back.

Take suicide talk seriously.

4. My twelve-year-old son has drugged me numerous times and tried to kill me. I'm not kidding. I can't live like this anymore. Help! He also leaves the pool gate open purposely, hoping to encourage our three-year-old daughter to go for a swim at the bottom of the pool. He has admitted his motives. I've worked through Preteen Wise *and a host of other books and courses. What can I do short of having him arrested and taken from our home?*

If you have a situation like this, you should immediately call social services to get a referral. Having your child arrested is probably not necessary at this point, but having him evaluated definitely is. Call your local mental health center. Talk to your clergy. Find out where you can get help. You are dealing with seriously destructive, disturbed behavior that needs immediate attention.

It's sad to say, but sometimes the best option is to have a child like this removed from the home for a while, especially if you fear for the safety of other children or yourself. An organization like Teen Challenge may be ideal to handle this situation.

You'll want to do some careful soul searching here. Children don't usually develop this kind of behavior by themselves. Often in cases like this, one or both parents are out of control. It may not only be the child who needs professional help.

SECTION 8: THE MEDIA, INTERNET AND COMPUTERS

1. I'm so fed up with my teenager's media choices that I'm just about ready to cancel cable, throw away the TV and the radio, break some CDs, and sell our computer. Before I go on my rampage, is there a better way to react?

When parents who now have teenagers began their parenting in the mid-1980s, they did not have the media pressure that is in force today. Back then, all we had in our homes were TVs and stereos. Now we've got multiple computers, all hooked to the Internet, VCRs and DVDs, big-screen TVs with surround sound THX speakers, console video games, palmtops, CD boom boxes, and remote controls by the dozen.

Who would have guessed that communications technology would advance so quickly? It's understandable that parents may feel they're coming late to the media game. However, that's where we are, and there's no going back. Your teenager may have many more ways to offend you with his media choices today, but in the end it's no different from the teen who shocked his parents by listening to rock 'n' roll on the radio in the fifties.

Is this your home? Are you still paying the mortgage? Are you still covering the insurance costs? Do you still put food on the table? Are there certain things that are offensive to you? Here again, parents, you need to get a backbone. You have a right to influence what your kids watch while they're in your house. Don't be afraid to apply some pressure to limit things that create destructive attitudes or patterns of behavior. You need to encourage some self-control and set some limitations.

When you do, it's very possible that your kids will welcome your restrictions. Every child grows in respect for parents who know how to take a stand at the right time, at the right place, in the right way.

2. My teenager plays video games from the moment he gets home from school until I force him to go to bed at night. I'm thinking things are a little out of control. Am I crazy, or could he be addicted to that thing?

Yes, it's very possible that this could be an addiction of sorts, especially if the teen has an obsessive kind of personality. The good news is that there is no physiological, chemical addiction involved.

If video games (or computer games or Internet time) have gotten out of control in your teen's life, especially if it's begun to impact other areas of behavior, it's time for you to intervene. Take away the privilege for a while. Work to help him regain his balance and redraw his priorities.

It's good for you and your teen both to know that certain things could become problems in the future. Awareness of the propensity should help you instill defenses against future addictive temptations when they come. There are good resources for computer and Internet addiction in books and on the Web.

3. Can the various forms of media be the source of our relational tension with our teen?

"My son's a media junkie," one mother said. "As soon as he gets up, he's got VH-1 turned on in his room. After breakfast he's on the computer. He says he's just checking his e-mail, but his little sister tells me that's not all he's doing. I can still hear the rap music pounding through the ground after his car has pulled out of the driveway. When he comes home from school, it's the same in reverse, with video games, band magazines, and the occasional almost X-rated movie thrown in, too.

"If I ever dare ask him to do a chore or spend time with the family, you would think that I'd asked him to cut off his hand. I don't mind music and movies and all, but I wish they didn't seem to be standing between him and me."

Today we live in the latter stages of the information revolution. Our lives are saturated with print and electronic media. If we let it, it will occupy every waking moment of our lives.

Though media choices come up in many parent/teen conflicts, we do not believe radio, movies, TV, magazines, the Internet, and the rest *cause* rebellion in teens. The offensive media choices teens make are usually symptoms of something deeper. However, we do believe the media of our culture feed rebellion and encourage its growth. Media's message is often subtly degrading. It can act to distance teens from their family's common moral stance, further deconstructing already unstable relationships.

Mass media, particularly that connected with the music scene, can provide an identity for a young person who hasn't been given one in his family. Without a family identity at home and a moral community reinforcing it, teens can feel they don't know who they are. Popular media provide an answer. Chances are, though, you won't be pleased with the identity your teenager adopts from MTV.

When parents begin to investigate media's role in relational tension between them and their teens, we always urge them to consider the context they have provided in their homes. Are parents bothered that their teens are watching near-porn on cable, but they think it's fine to let them watch R-rated movies that depict sexual activity? Are parents upset that their teens are investigating the occult, but they don't bat an eyelid when they play with preoccult toys or games like *Magic: The Gathering, Pokémon,* and *Dungeons & Dragons*? Parents who establish a certain tolerance for immorality in the home shouldn't be surprised when their teens just want to take the next logical step. That statement is not meant to accuse but to point out that a little leaven leavens the whole lump.

Another thing to guard against is trying to make common tastes, rather than common values, the foundation for family identity. Whenever parents try to make their teens conform to a fixed set of preferences, they are almost guaranteed relational tension in the home. Is it really so bad that you like opera and your daughter likes ska? It would be ridiculous for parents to demand that their children all prefer the color green over any other color. In the same way, to demand that all favor the same tastes in music, movies, and dress would be to beg for conflict.

Virtues and morals, not enforced media preferences, ought to form the basis for a family's common ground. The greater the shared common values among family members, the less likely teenagers' preferences will scare you. Unite yourselves on the basis of values or else you will forever battle preferences and tastes in friends, music, clothing, and the rest.

14

Dating, Courtship and Marriage

There is no doubt that if you have a teen in your home the issue of dating has already been a topic of discussion. How should you be directing your child's thinking on this subject?

In spite of the information and pressures your teen will receive from those around him, it is important that you direct your teen's thinking on the issue. God has placed you in a position of great influence over your children. As such, you create healthy, and sometimes not-so-healthy expectations by the promises you make. The child at thirteen that hears, "You can date at sixteen," will expect to do so. Most teens will even remind you on their sixteenth birthday of your long-ago promise. "Okay, I'm sixteen. Now I can date." Be careful what you promise for the future. Sixteen is going to come quickly enough and by the time your child gets there you will probably be sorry you set any age for dating. To understand the dynamics of courtship and dating, it will be helpful to return to the Bible and first century Judaism.

COURTSHIP, DATING AND THE BIBLE

Should your teen date? What about peer pressure and the expectations of friends? What about courtship? Can we make a biblical case for or against dating and courtship? Let's talk about the wisdom of courting and the practice of dating.

Actually, the Bible doesn't offer specific guidelines for courtship and dating, although courtship (and probably dating, to some extent) was practiced by the Jews in the first century. The only marriage custom spoken of in the Bible was betrothment, meaning to pledge to marry or to become engaged.

The word "betroth" speaks of a marriage commitment of a son or daughter. It appears throughout the Law of Moses (Exodus 21:8-9; Leviticus 19:20; Deuteronomy 22:25, 28:30) and is also used poetically by the prophets. God speaking through Hosea said, "I will betroth you to Me forever; Yes, I will betroth you to Me in righteousness and justice, in loving kindness and mercy. I will betroth you to Me in faithfulness, and you shall know the Lord" (Hosea 2:19-20).

If you look for a definitive statement in the Bible on the methods and timing of betrothment or courtship, you will not find one. There is no biblical injunction governing these activities. What we know of these practices comes from the study of early Jewish customs. (Jewish customs should not be viewed as a substitute for biblical revelation.) Jewish historians considered betrothment to be a formal act of property transfer wherein the groom gave his bride money or something else of monetary value to secure her.

In return, someone from the bride's family (usually the father) gave a written declaration, which became known as the marriage contract. Although it has no biblical commendation, the "marriage contract" containing the "marriage agreement" has survived two millenniums. In 1828, Noah Webster's American Dictionary of the English Language defined "betroth" as "a contract for future marriage, done either by a father for his daughter or by a man contracting a future wife."

Anne Marie's grandmother's betrothal contract of April 13, 1906, notarized in Boston, Massachusetts, hangs on the wall in our upstairs bedroom. In it, Anne Marie Salza of Avellino Province, Italy agreed to marry Pietro Perrino of Boston, Massachusetts when she came to America. Both parties signed the contract. The contract clause of betrothal survived into the 1940s where it appeared in 1942 in the Webster Consolidated Dictionary. Over the next twenty years, however, the popular meaning of betrothment, with the marriage contract clause, began to change. By the mid-1960s the contract element was dropped in many dictionaries, returning the word to its original Hebrew meaning: an agreement to marry—to be engaged.

DATING AND COURTSHIP

In 1828 Noah Webster defined dating as, "knowing the time of happening or to assign a date to an event or letter." Now, approximately a hundred seventy-five years later, modern dictionaries define dating as "a social engagement with persons of the opposite sex." The fact that teens didn't date a hundred seventy-five years ago does not make dating wrong–just different from times past. Dating must be judged on its merits, not on its existence.

We won't say that dating itself is wrong, but we will say that sometimes the contemporary context of dating creates conditions that could be hurtful to young people. What makes dating acceptable or unacceptable is the age of participants, the appropriateness of the relationship, the context of dating, and the motive for dating.

The question isn't whether or not dating is bad, but whether it creates a false expectation of commitment that can never be fulfilled. We think it can, especially when it gets into the boyfriend/girlfriend stage. Teenagers are expected to commit to a monogamous relationship that is designed to be temporary. How can this reinforce the idea that marriage is designed to be a *permanent* monogamous relationship?

Young people are giving away their hearts too early, then having them broken. They're getting their emotions stirred, then having them trampled. When you consider the pressure from peer groups for teen couples to get involved sexually, the whole idea of dating seems less advisable than ever.

It used to be that the common moral community acted as a de facto chaperon. There was social and peer pressure to act properly on a date. Today peer pressure doesn't keep teenagers away from sex, it pushes them toward it.

One popular alternative to one-on-one dating is group dating. Our own daughters went out every Friday night with four or five of their friends. The members of the group were from homes within our moral community, so we knew the teens would share a moral standard we approved of. They had as much fun and probably more fun than if they'd gone out with just one person. One reason this was attractive to them was that they realized, as young people are realizing today, that at age seventeen or eighteen or nineteen, they weren't wanting to get married. Why establish a long-term relationship with someone if neither party is ready for marriage?

DATING VS. COURTSHIP

Dating, as the word is used today, implies a casual, recreational relationship between two people who usually have no intention of marrying each other anytime soon. It can be a very useful and fun way of extending friendships and exploring compatibility. It's a way for morally mature young people to find out the kinds of things they like and don't like in members of the opposite sex, helping them refine what they're looking for in a future spouse.

As we said above, we have nothing against the idea of dating, per se. What we object to is the environment of dating in which teens are urged to engage in sexual activity. We can applaud parents who decide to encourage restrictions on their teenagers' dating, and we trust those who allow their teens to date (though we hope they lay out some clear parameters for their teens).

At the same time, we do think group dating is a great alternative for both groups. It retains the benefits of dating, having fun and exploring compatibility, and the group of like-minded teens acts as a source of positive peer pressure, reinforcing moral behavior for all its members.

There are special occasions in which datelike arrangements might be appropriate. One of the Ezzo daughters elected to go to her ninth grade banquet. She dined in the beautifully decorated school gymnasium with the rest of her class. The young man who accompanied her was not her *date* so much as her *escort* for the evening. It was a fun event, but a one time occurrence. There was no commitment on either side for beyond that evening. For everything else, we recommend either group dating or courtship.

Courtship refers to a type of activity whose goal is marriage. It is the attempt on the part of a young man to win the affections of a young woman's heart, with the express purpose of entering into matrimony. Courtship was the primary method of wooing in previous centuries until it was replaced by dating sometime after World War II. There's no reason courtship can't be revived, and in fact, we are seeing a resurgence of the practice already.

We fully realize that courtship is not for everybody. What we describe may strike you as highly ideal. If your daughter has just had her boyfriend's name, Snake, tattooed on her chin, the thought that they might enter formal courtship might give you a good laugh. But read this section anyway. You may find that you like what you see and decide to adapt it to your situation, if not in Snake's case, then maybe for your younger children.

Apples and Oranges: Dating and Courtship Compared

As we have demonstrated already, courting and dating are not synonymous. Here are some important differences to think about. First, courtship requires age-readiness for marriage. Dating, on the other hand, usually allows younger teens premature access to the type of committed, male/female relationship that should be reserved for courtship and marriage. This can be very damaging emotionally. The frequent comings and goings of boyfriend/girlfriend relationships do not engender stability, but self-doubt and fragility. Because many teens do not yet have the skills to keep their emotions in check, dating can open the door for all kinds of exploitation, from being taken advantage of financially and socially to surrendering oneself sexually.

Second, courtship presupposes the possibility of a mature love relationship that will lead to engagement. Dating makes no such assumption. Most kids date because they're looking for a good time in the here and now. They have come to expect a level of entertainment from a dating partner. But if the fun runs dry, teens don't drop dating, they drop their date. They look for someone new to please them. We believe this builds wrong expectations for marriage. Because courtship is not so transitory, it is a better preparation for marriage.

Third, courtship considers factors beyond just the couple, such as parents, family and extended family, belief systems, values, and personal convictions. Consideration is given to how a couple's decisions might affect other important relationships. Not so with dating, which is confined to a single, narrow activity—the date itself. What takes place between the pickup and drop-off is the only thing that really matters to the dating couple.

Fourth, courtship is a means to an end: engagement. Dating is an end unto itself. The emphasis in dating is usually present and momentary satisfaction, not the possibility of choosing a spouse or preparing for marriage.

Courtship, then, is the prelude to a possible engagement. Its purpose is to provide a couple with time to discover, assess, and evaluate their compatibility as potential lifelong marriage partners. Courtship isn't a time of experimentation but of exploration.

Courtship is not a guarantee of engagement but a measured step toward it. Both the couple involved in the relationship and their parents have the freedom to pull the reins if things are not going as they should. The closer two people grow together, the more the underlying (and not necessarily pleasant) habits begin to show themselves. That's why neither teens nor parents should rush toward courtship without some mechanism for stopping the process.

THE THREE PHASES OF COURTSHIP

Courtship naturally unfolds in three phases: exploration, confirmation, and pledging. Each phase brings a new level of responsibility and unique challenges to the couple, and each phase allows for either person to pull in the reins and slow down the process.

There is no set time limit for these phases. Couples will pass through each phase on a timetable unique to their relational needs and expectations. There are a variety of factors that will influence the length of each phase, including the maturity of the couple, parental favor, and the comfort level of the couple themselves.

Phase One: Exploration

Courtship is not for young teens. It is for older teens (or twenty-somethings or beyond) who are of an age and a maturity level at which they can rightly consider marriage. Nor is courtship for strangers. Your son or daughter should only enter into a courtship relationship with someone who is already a good friend. Best friends make the best spouses. If a young man and woman know they get along well, it's natural for them to take the next step. Entering into courtship is acknowledging that marriage is a possibility but not a promise.

The first phase of courtship is an exploratory phase. Its purpose is to allow the couple to discover and explore their emotions for each other beyond the level of simple friendship. Their commitments are forming and being tried out. Each learns to rearrange his or her life for the benefit of the other. Each begins to understand the give-and-take necessary to meet the other person's needs while still getting his or her own needs met. They enjoy the pleasant aspects of each other's personalities, discovering wonderful things they never knew. They also discover not-so-wonderful things they never knew. They find out whether they can live with those things or if it's just too much.

Phase Two: Confirmation

Now it starts to heat up in the kitchen. Some of the starry-eyed romance is giving way to the unspectacular reality. The couple is faced with the dilemma of self-revelation: They want to show more of their own secret selves, but they're afraid of rejection. Here, as they tentatively allow their courtship partner into their secret places and as they watch how the other person reacts, they start to become sure that this is (or isn't) *the one*.

During the process of confirmation, the couple learns how to overcome frustrations, jealousies, insecurities, and misunderstandings. This is the in-the-trenches phase of courtship. Many relationships do not survive it. But it's better for a couple to find out now that they're not compatible than in engagement or marriage.

Those couples who emerge from this phase still able to smile and gaze lovingly into each other's eyes are marvelously confirmed in their relationship. They now have actual evidence that their relationship isn't just built on bubbly infatuation. They have taken a close look at one another, seen the other person, warts and all, and still decided to remain committed.

This process doesn't end in marriage. There are some things that will never be revealed until two people actually live together. But the best that can be hoped for before then is a good, hard look at the other person. If the relationship can survive that, the couple has sufficient confidence in the expression of each other's love to declare the relationship publicly.

Phase Three: Engagement

The next logical step is for the man to approach the woman's father to ask for her hand in marriage. During this phase, the couple achieves a marriage of their souls that only awaits the calendar date.

So many marriages do not last. So many married couples have tension with one or both sets of in-laws. So many get into marriage before they really take a close look at their future spouse. All of these problems and more can be avoided through courtship.

READY FOR WEDDING BELLS?

Let's say you didn't know about courtship. Your teenager has been in a serious dating relationship for a long time, maybe years. They're talking about marriage. How can you know if they're ready? In this day of no-fault divorces and multiple marriages, you want your child's marriage to be able to withstand the fires of real life. So how can you know?

We believe that a couple is ready to consider marriage when they have reached maturity in three key areas: life-management skills, moral/social maturity, and compatibility discovery. Let's look at each one.

Life-Management Skills

A child is ready for marriage (or courtship) if he or she can manage basic life skills apart from Mom and Dad's supervision. A son or daughter must be able to handle the rigors of married life, including selfless care for another person. Both girls and boys must know how to prepare a meal, wash clothes, set a table, make wise purchases, manage finances, maintain employment that can sustain a family, and care for children.

Marriage is no place to start learning these basic life-management skills. Hopefully, you've been teaching these skills to your children all along.

Moral/Social Maturity

Among the most important developmental tasks to be achieved prior to marriage is the attainment of a moral/social maturity. Once a couple is married, neither one should be expecting to run home to Mommy when times get hard.

Before being ready for marriage, young people need to reach a level of social maturity that will allow them to function in an adult community. They need social adeptness in order to govern the dynamics of an adult relationship, especially a marital relationship. Think about your teenager: Does he or she behave like an adult in social settings? If not, better think about delaying the wedding.

Marriage will bring testing, conflicts, stress, and financial strain. No matter how long they've been courting or dating, there will always be an eye-opening period of discovery when each partner realizes things about the other that had so far remained concealed. There will be pressure from work, advice from in-laws, and obligations of responsible citizenship.

Marriage is hard. Immature young people need not apply.

Compatibility Discovery

Many marriage problems result from couples not taking this component of marriage preparation seriously. Compatibility discovery is the process of investigating the proposed marriage partner to determine his or her suitability for marriage. There are two noteworthy facts regarding marital compatibility. First, one does not *become* compatible with a mate. You're either compatible or you're not. True compatibility is discovered not learned.

Second, compatibility cannot be discovered if either party has not achieved basic life-management skills or moral/social maturity. A potential marriage partner who can't remember to pay bills or who expects Daddy to come and fix everything is not a compatible marriage partner for anyone.

The Seven Levels of Compatibility Discovery

Stone quarries use gravel shakers to separate stones of various sizes. As crushed stone passes through smaller and smaller filters, each screen in a sense becomes the doorkeeper allowing passage for the purer and finer particles.

So it is with compatibility discovery in a couple. There are "compatibility screens" that allow or prevent deeper development in the relationship. As the two people pass through each screen, they grow closer and become more familiar and comfortable with their similarities and differences. If they decide to stop at any point, it would not destroy a friendship but would merely halt its progress at that level. These screens' purpose is to allow truly compatible couples to proceed with confidence and to halt ill-suited couples' progression toward a type of intimacy discovery reserved for marriage.

LEVEL ONE: AT-LARGE SOCIAL COMPATIBILITY

At-large social compatibility means the couple notices each other from a distance. Perhaps they see each other at a party or in class. They are simply attracted to one another.

One of the Ezzo's son-in-law Paul and his daughter Jennifer first noticed each other while working together on a church project. Generally speaking, the two had certain things in common. They were both committed to their church, they both enjoyed sports, and they were both active in youth ministry. It was in that public context that a general social compatibility was established.

It was a broad rapport, almost an absence of negatives rather than a presence of positives. Neither one did anything in public that caused the other to wish he or she were somewhere else. From a distance, they both recognized a general similarity that naturally encouraged them to move to the next level.

LEVEL TWO: GENERAL PERSONALITY COMPATIBILITY

It wasn't long after they met that both Paul and Jennifer realized how much they enjoyed working together. They appreciated each other's humor and moments of seriousness. Working together afforded them opportunities to witness the strengths and weaknesses of each other's personality. They found they enjoyed similar group projects, responded to certain situations the same way, and enjoyed many of the same leisure activities.

It was at this point that they began group dating. Paul and Jennifer would often go out with some of the youth leaders for meals after their ministry times.

LEVEL THREE: FRIENDSHIP COMPATIBILITY

No male/female relationship should even begin leaning toward marriage until after a friendship has been established. Therefore courtship should not begin until a real friendship is present.

Both kids discovered that they shared common values and goals. They enjoyed similar activities outside the context of youth work. They started doing fun little things for each other, such as when a lunch was shared with the one who forgot to bring theirs. Or when Jennifer baked Paul's favorite cookies for the all-boys weekend campout.

It was after they had developed this friendship compatibility that Paul approached Gary and Anne Marie for permission to move to the first phase of courtship. He was doing more than asking to date his daughter: He was seeking approval to begin courting her, which meant he was wanting to investigate the possibility of marrying her. In so doing, they moved into the exploration phase of courtship.

If the relationship continued to progress, he would eventually need to come to Gary again to ask for her hand in marriage.

LEVEL FOUR: MORAL AND INTELLECTUAL COMPATIBILITY

Once friendship compatibility is established, it quickly leads to the discovery of moral and intellectual compatibility, especially if the couple is in a courtship mode.

Not only did Paul and Jennifer enjoy similar fun activities while in each other's company, but they began to discover how each other viewed the world. That came by way of discovering each other's personal level of integrity and how each lived out his or her convictions. It also exposed their own intellectual skills as they discussed various issues of social and political theory and their general worldviews.

If there had been a major disagreement between them at this phase, something they could not seem to resolve no matter what, they might have decided to break off the courtship. Better to find out then that they were philosophically antithetical than to find out after the wedding. But their friendship would hopefully have remained.

LEVEL FIVE: FAMILY COMPATIBILITY

Couples are usually discovering family compatibility at the same time as they're discovering moral and intellectual compatibility. In this phase, each member of the couple is trying to see if there is a fit with the other's family.

During this time, Paul started to drop by the Ezzos' house more often. He participated in family nights, went out to dinner with them on occasion, and helped with a few household projects. The Ezzos were getting to know him as a family, and he was getting a glimpse into how things worked in Jennifer's family. By this time, too, Jennifer had become a household name with Paul's family.

It was at this point that Paul and Jennifer's relationship moved to the next level. It's a wonderful thing to see the man or woman of your dreams accepted heartily by your family. Paul approached Gary a second time to update him about how he and Jennifer were maturing in their love for one another. He voluntarily sought Gary's blessing to allow him to continue pursuing Jennifer, and Gary gave it.

LEVEL SIX: PRIVATE WORLD COMPATIBILITY

It is at this level that one's capacity to be intimate is realized. Not physical intimacy, of course, but a type that is much more important for marriage: the intimacy of souls. During this phase each partner steps out to reveal his or her heart, complete with its fears and follies and moments of irrationality.

It's risky to be vulnerable to anyone, especially the person you may spend the rest of your life with. But when the other person treats you with compassion, you learn to trust, and you'll be likely to share further vulnerabilities later. There is nothing so wonderful as a marriage partner who knows you fully yet loves you anyway.

When Paul found that Jennifer could be trusted with his deepest fears and insecurities, and vice versa, they knew they were ready to commit to marriage. Paul came to Gary again and asked permission to continue pursuing Jennifer as his wife. If he was nervous about approaching Gary the first time, by the third time it was an easy thing.

LEVEL SEVEN: SYNERGY COMPATIBILITY

In terms of marriage, synergy is present when the interaction of two individuals causes their life together to be greater than the sum of their lives apart. This phase isn't concerned so much with what the couple needs to discover about one another, but rather with what they realize about themselves as a team.

To succeed at this level, each should find that he or she is completed by the other. A husband should make his wife's endeavors far more successful than they were when she was on her own. A husband with a good wife will find himself capable of unimagined heights. That's synergy in a marriage. If it is not evident in the engagement, the couple needs to reconsider their plans. But if synergy is there, it's the final confirmation that the marriage will be what it is designed to be. Synergy compatibility allows the image of intimacy to be realized in its fullness.

It was at this point that Paul came to Gary a fourth time: to ask for Jennifer's hand in marriage. Five months later they were married.

Compatibility discovery is crucial before a couple says "I do." These seven layers of ever finer screens will ensure that problems are surfaced before vows are made—and, if no problems are identified during this time, a couple will gain great confidence to enter married life together.

STEPPING ON THE BRAKES

If at any point in the courtship, either member of the couple *or* either family had had misgivings about the relationship, they could have brought those up. That's the beauty of courtship over dating: There is a circle of advisors around the couple, people who can sometimes see things the person in the situation can't.

At one point in Jennifer and Paul's courtship, Jennifer began having hesitations about the relationship. With her parents support, Jennifer decided to take a month off. It was not an easy time for either Paul or Jennifer, but necessary. At the end of the month, Jennifer and Paul's love for each other was confirmed, and the courtship went forward at mach one.

We can probably all think of couples who got married but shouldn't have. If only they'd had the protection the courtship structure would have provided them. Your teen isn't just marrying the person he's dating, he's marrying that whole family. A courtship framework can prove the truth of the old saying, "In the abundance of counselors there is victory."

I'M SAVING MYSELF

Throughout compatibility discovery, courtship or dating, and engagement, sexual purity is of greatest importance. Nothing can sabotage the marriage bed more effectively than guilt over premarital sex. And nothing is so beautiful as a pure man and woman coming together on their wedding night to consummate a marriage.

Though our society says a young man's not a man yet until he's had sex and a young woman who doesn't put out is a prude, it isn't so. That's just the voice of insecure people wanting others to validate their mistakes by repeating them. Encourage your teenager to remain sexually pure until marriage.

In a sense, even a young child is already married: He or she is promised to his or her future spouse. His or her wedding gift is remaining sexually pure for that person until the wedding night. Years before your child says "I do" at his or her wedding, he or she should have made sincere vows to that future bride or groom. It is an oath of faithfulness to remain sexually pure, given to the marriage partner in absentia.

How can you help your children succeed in this area? What can you do in a noncoercive way to encourage their purity and remind them of their pledge? Here is a beautiful example of how one father helped his daughter guard her heart for marriage and her future mate. While the daughter's age in this story is thirteen, other parents who have used this method have waited until their daughters were fifteen or sixteen.

On the occasion of her thirteenth birthday, a father planned a special date with his daughter. He wanted their time together to be so special that it would be almost impossible for his daughter to forget it. The father's purpose for the grand evening was to encourage her to commit herself to sexual purity during her teen years. He had planned this special date for months, and now everything was ready.

Early on the morning of the special day, the girl's mother presented her with a gold key, along with instructions to give the key as a gift to her father after he had given his gift to her. The mother assured her that she would then understand why she was to give away her birthday present.

That evening, the father arrived in a chauffeur-driven Mercedes to pick up his daughter. She was nervous about her first "date," but excited. The ride to the restaurant was filled with light, enjoyable conversation as father and daughter recounted many fun memories.

After a marvelous dinner, the father told his daughter that he wanted the very best for her life. He explained that she would be facing many new challenges in the years to come, one of which would be developing relationships with boys. He explained that, as her father, he had been given the joy and responsibility of watching over her and protecting her, especially during the teen years. Then he asked her to make a commitment that she would allow him to do that, to watch over her and protect her during her teen years.

At that moment, the father pulled out his gift and gave it to her. Inside, she found a beautiful gold heart on a gold chain. As the father placed the chain around her neck, he explained that the gold heart represented her sexual purity. He asked her if she had something for him. She remembered the key her mother had given her, and she brought it out. Before she could hand it to him, her father told her that by doing so she would be saying, "Yes, Dad, I want you to have the key to my heart, to protect it and keep it safe until marriage."

The father, understandably happy, made a promise to his little girl: "I will guard the key to your heart and all that it represents until the day of your wedding. Then I will give it to your husband."

If you have a son, you can adapt this ceremony for him. It's a little more complicated, but it accomplishes the same thing. After we describe our suggestion, you may be able to come up with a way that works better for you.

Use a woman's necklace and a man's ring for a boy. Mom and Dad take their son to dinner. Dad gives his son the necklace, which the boy then gives to the first woman in his life: his mother. She promises to keep it as a reminder of his pledge of purity and commitment to the girl who will someday be his wife. In exchange, Mom gives her son a gold ring engraved with the date of his pledge. The son is to wear the ring as a reminder of his vow of purity to his future wife.

On her son's wedding day, if the boy has abstained, the mother gives the necklace to the bride, symbolizing the fulfillment of his pledge. The son gives the ring to his father-in-law and mother-in-law, signifying his personal commitment to their daughter. (Or you could choose to use the ring in the construction of the wedding band.)

It is neither the ceremony nor the objects involved that assure commitment to these vows, but the steady, loving encouragement from Mom and Dad. Whether it be for a daughter or son, the locket, ring, and necklace are only reminders of a pledge. You are the most significant force in insuring that your child comes to his or her wedding in sexual purity.

SUMMARY

We don't believe it is best for teens to become involved in the dating experience outside of courtship. Dating, as it is usually defined today, can very often lead to improper intimacy, temporary relationships, and sexual experimentation, not to mention teenage pregnancy, AIDS, or abortion.

Not only is that not healthy for the person involved, it also defrauds the future mate. For too many teens, dating is like sampling a box of chocolates: They take a bite out of as many as they can, making them all undesirable for anyone who comes after.

In a sense, parents are custodians of their children. We are their managers or guardians. Think of someone who has been charged with delivering a custom-made car to its new owner. It seems the world itself rises up to damage that car: Rust, flying pebbles, salt air, other cars, criminals, and paint-scratching delinquents all work to spoil the beauty of what you're handling. So it is your task to give that car defenses against the elements and protect it from those who would hurt it so that you can present it to its rightful owner in pristine condition.

Instill in your teenager a passion for purity–purity in his or her own body and a demand for purity in the life of his or her future mate.

Questions For Review

1. How do you feel about letting your teenager date? What restrictions, if any, do you feel are appropriate?

2. Do you think courtship, as the authors described it, is too radical for your family? What elements of the idea of courtship would you like to incorporate for your own teen?

3. What is the primary difference between dating and courtship, and how do you feel about it?

4. What are the three phases of courtship?

5. What, if anything, would you add to the authors' list of what a teen must display before being ready for marriage?

A Final Thought

I f there is one word that can sum up a final charge to our readers, it is the word *discovery*. Here is a story told by a friend that summarizes our final point.

"Back in the early 70's, my family lived in Hong Kong. As a hobby, my parents enjoyed finding and refinishing antiques. Sunday afternoons were often spent visiting a place commonly referred to as "Cat Street." It was at this Chinese flea market that we were able to rummage amongst the discards of the local people in search of unknown treasures.

One day, while on one of our excursions, we came upon a room divider screen. It had several panels which folded up accordion style. In the center panels of the framed screen was a mural depicting a scenic view of a portion of the great wall of China. The outermost portions of the segmented screen contained Chinese caricatures. However, it was obvious by looking at the screen that it had been poorly cared for. The years of neglect were reflected in its condition. The frames of the screen were soiled with the fading power of grime, smoke, and time. The glass within the frames covering the mural had become so obscure and cloudy that the image beneath was blurred and distorted. The years of exposure to the elements of the world had caused the screen to fade. Even the fabric on which the mural was placed was either stained or had begun to deteriorate and rot. Still, my parents for some odd reason took a fancy to this discarded remnant and brought it home to clean up.

When we got home, we began to wipe off the grime from the piece. It was then that we could see that the mural beneath the glass was actually an embroidery. The drab olive gray landscape of the Chinese hillside, now discernible, was actually a fine piece of art work accomplished through the needlepoint of a very skilled craftsman. Although time had taken its toll on the work, the handiwork of the artist was still visible.

With great excitement, we worked to remove the embroidered panels from the frames. As my father cautiously removed the wooden back of the first panel, I can still recall our amazement at what we saw. For as my father removed the back of the panel, the color of the original embroidery threads exploded with vivid brilliance to depict the richness of the original tapestry. The treasure within yielded up the splendor of vibrant colors that depicted life itself. Protected and sheltered within the confines of the framework, the elements of the world were unable to deteriorate the magnificence of the original working. In awe we looked at the beauty of the work in its original form just as it was on the day it was sealed.

Frame by frame we worked to clean the screen, seeing for the first time the glowing beauty of the art work from the back side of each panel. Each panel was breathtaking on its own account, yet collectively they formed a majestic scene of the great wall of China. So, after dismantling the portions of the screen displaying the mural, we began to clean the outside panels with the Chinese caricatures. We asked our Chinese housekeeper to interpret their meaning. She responded by giving us the following translation. 'Mr. Shald, the characters say:

It takes strong marriages to build strong families.
It takes strong families to build strong people.
It takes strong people to build a strong nation.'"

There are many families all around us stained by the world and dulled by time. For some the original sketch of a beautiful family is so faded that it cannot even be imagined. Maybe your family is like the outside of the mural in this story. But like that mural, stained and discolored by the grime of the world, there lies just beneath the surface a beautiful piece of handiwork. It waits to be discovered by loving eyes and caring hands who are willing to work to reveal its secrets. The hidden tapestry of the Christian family has a brilliance within, woven by Calvary's love, infused with a heavenly radiance. Discover the beauty of your family, and let the world see the Master's handiwork.

Appendix

The Myth About the
Myth of Adolescence

It has been suggested that defining the period of adolescence and applying it socially to our teens, is the actual root cause of teen-parent conflict. Although this view is held by only a small portion of the clinical population, it does warrant some comment. The premise is best stated this way: Adolescence is an artificial secondary stage of development thrust upon twentyfirst-century man by the industrial revolution. As such, it only serves to reinforce delayed maturity in children. The myth of adolescence, as this view is commonly referred to, presupposes that delayed maturity is bad for children and is the probable cause of teen rebellion. But in order to exist, this view forces a redefinition of the words maturity and adulthood by removing them from their normative, historical, biological, intellectual, and moral usage. Does a child become an adult when he matures, or does he mature when he becomes an adult? What is maturity? What is adulthood?

Growing up has more than one aspect to it. Before we can put the challenge of adolescence into perspective, we first must look at the four classes of maturity–legal, physical, social/intellectual, and moral. How a society views these four levels of maturity highly influences how they view adolescence in general.

Legal Maturity

Legal maturity is defined by statute or by custom, not by experience. Every people group in the world follows some generally accepted guideline which marks a child's "rite of passage" into adulthood. This is typically a rather formal definition and marks the child's inclusion into the adult community with all its rights and responsibilities.

For example, in America most states allow a sixteen- year-old the legal right to drive a car. But that same sixteen-year-old cannot legally vote until he is eighteen. He can legally play the California lottery as an eighteen-year-old, but he cannot legally buy alcoholic beverages until he is twenty-one.

Of course, the mere passage of time does not signal maturity at all levels. We know that "legal age" does not necessarily indicate that a teen is adult-like emotionally, socially, financially, or spiritually. Yet in a legal sense, the child is now an adult.

Physical Maturity

All humans of every tongue, tribe, and nation have the same patterns of physical growth and development. As a result, every person reaches physical maturity at approximately the same time. Physical growth is rapid during infancy and early childhood, followed by a slower pace just before puberty. A spurt of rapid growth follows puberty, extending into mid-adolescence; then it plateaus and slows down until adulthood.

Between eighteen and twenty years of age, the skeletal growth process ends. This is marked by two events: the achievement of maximum body growth (height) and ossification of the sacral bones. Physical maturity, then, is marked both by the attainment of maximum growth and the cessation of growth.

Social/Intellectual Maturity

Legal adulthood is fairly objective. A child reaches a prescribed age assigned by the society and he is declared "legally of age." Physical maturity also can be objectively observed. In contrast, social/intellectual maturity has no such benchmark but is highly influenced by each society.

To explain this class of maturity, we'll begin by defining the terms "social maturity" and "intellectual maturity." Social maturity refers to one's readiness to be an active participant in social policy and the good of the society at large. Intellectual maturity speaks to the minimum level of intellectual and academic attainment necessary to function in the adult community. From those two definitions, it can be said that the level of social/intellectual maturity required before one can enter the adult community is determined by the simplicity or complexity of each society.

Every society sets its own minimum social/intellectual standard that must be met before a person is accepted as an adult. This basic law establishes the length of adolescence within every society. As parents, we can gain important insights by taking a look at this basic law in four different cultural settings: primitive-tribal, pre- and mid-industrial America, post-modern America, and historical Judaism.

PRIMITIVE/TRIBAL SOCIETIES

Anthropologists who worked with primitive tribes showed that in such societies children can pass directly from childhood into adulthood without going through an adolescence phase. This happens because preparation for adulthood in such settings presents few of the social, intellectual, or moral challenges that are common to advanced societies. We have personally witnessed the social/intellectual phenomenon in primitive settings. Many of the skills needed to participate in the adult community—for example, fishing, hunting and crop planting are actually gained before the onset of puberty. Primitive simplicity does not move children into adulthood earlier but brings adult status closer in age to childhood. This last point is further demonstrated by examining adolescence in pre-industrial America.

PRE- AND MID-INDUSTRIAL AMERICA

The social and intellectual skills needed to participate as an adult a hundred years ago were far less demanding than they are today. At the turn of the twentieth century, it was not uncommon for girls and boys to marry at fourteen or fifteen years of age and set up housekeeping. A simpler life meant a simpler transition into adulthood and a shorter period of adolescence. This does not mean children back then matured sooner, but rather what was required for social and intellectual maturity was far less demanding than today.

POST-MODERN AMERICA

The phrase "post-modern America" is a relatively new societal classification that marks another level of social/intellectual advancement. Today, we live in the Age of Information. This term speaks to the volumes of current knowledge available to the average constituents. Both the volume and complexity of new information highly influences the length of adolescence in our day.

We live in an age of microchip technology. We talk of cyberspace, virtual reality, fiber optics, web sites, multi-tasking, and gigabytes. Adulthood in America, along with our European and Asian industrialized counterparts, requires the attainment of a variety of sophisticated skills and abilities unimagined just fifty years ago. The very complexity of the American adult life evokes a type of moratorium on early entry into adulthood. That's why a period of adolescent ripening is absolutely necessary in our current day. There is simply too much to learn. Society does not have confidence to allow a fifteen-year-old to drive a bus, fly a commercial airliner, handle the rigors of an emergency room doctor or public school teacher, compete in the bond market, design bridges, build skyscrapers, or handle a thousand other intellectually demanding and skill-intensive jobs.

The intricacies of modern adulthood will not allow teenagers to participate on an equal footing with adults. Adolescents lack a type of wisdom and judgment that is gained through time with age and experience. The period of adolescence in our post-modern America is necessary to better prepare our teens to compete effectively as adults in our society and world.

HISTORICAL JUDAISM

The "youth" phase in historical Judaism linked childhood with adulthood. It was a secondary phase very similar in nature to the adolescent phase found in pre-industrial America. In Bible times, maturity was not synonymous with adulthood. That distinction is important to grasp.

A minor reached "maturity" at thirteen, but adulthood came later, usually at around eighteen to twenty years of age. Maturity in the Hebrew culture spoke of a mixture of certain legal rights and moral obligations. It was a time when a child entered the adult world as a participant in religious and social ceremonies.

The Jewish Bar Mitzvah (which refers to the time when one becomes a son of the Mosaic Law) served this purpose for boys. It marked the beginning of a youth's independent legal status and the age of moral responsibility. At this point, a youth became a moral equal with his parents. He could legally buy and trade in the marketplace, be a witness in court, and even be married; but he was not "adult enough" to sell inherited real estate (the minimum age for such matters as this was eighteen), nor could he be a judge until he was twenty-one.

Biblically, God defined adulthood in Numbers 14:29. This Old Testament passage is the only narrative in Scripture that speaks to the age of adult accountability. You may remember that God declared those twenty years of age and older (except for Caleb and Joshua) would die in the wilderness for their sin of unbelief. The punishment was pronounced on the "adult population."

An examination of social/intellectual maturity in four different cultural settings makes one thing clear: The parameters of adolescence are governed by the adult demands of the culture in which an individual lives. The simpler the society, the sooner a child moves into adulthood. The more complex it is, the longer the adolescent transition. This is true of our society. That is why we believe that the period of adolescence is not a myth but a necessary reality.

Moral Maturity

It is natural to think that moral maturity follows the same growth patterns as does physical or social/intellectual maturity. Many assume that, since a child tends to mature in each of these categories just before entrance to adulthood, personal morality follows suit. This is not so. Such thinking actually delays moral maturity by removing from parents a sense of urgency. Childhood is the period for imparting moral instruction and directing moral training, but please note that adolescence is when principles of right living, thinking, and acting should be realized. In a biblical context, moral maturity (thinking and acting in harmony with God's moral law) should show itself between the ages of thirteen and fifteen.

By the time children reach the teen years, they should have begun acquiring a moral code to which they adhere with increasing frequency. Adherence is dependent upon three things: moral knowledge (what does God's moral law say?), moral reason (what does the law mean?), and parental example (how valid is the law in the life of those insisting on it?). Moral maturity means your teen not only knows right from wrong, but he or she knows *why* right is right and wrong is wrong.

If these three steps can be achieved in your home, a great family experience will be yours. Why? Because the greatest influence on relationships are the values of the heart. Common values unify; conflicting values war against intimate healthy relationships, especially in the teen years.

You want your teen to be your moral equal long before he or she reaches adulthood physically, socially, or intellectually. The decision to be honest is the same whether a teen makes it during a geometry test or an adult makes it when turning in an expense report. The fact that adults and teens are both on the same page morally forms the basis of *Along the Adolescent Way*.

Index